The G.I. Joe of Genesis

What God-Inspired Joseph Teaches Us About Dreams, Forgiveness, and Finishing Strong

David Rutherford

Unless otherwise stated, Scripture is taken from the Holy Bible, New International Version ®. Copyright © 1973, 1978, 1984 by International Bible Society. Used by permission of Zondervan Publishing House. All rights reserved.

Scripture quotations marked (NLT) are taken from the Holy Bible, New Living Translation, copyright © 1996, 2004, 2015 by Tyndale House Foundation. Used by permission of Tyndale House Publishers, Inc., Carol Stream, Illinois 60188. All rights reserved.

Sermon To Book
www.sermontobook.com

The G.I. Joe of Genesis / David Rutherford
ISBN-13: 978-1-952602-25-2

I dedicate this book to my father, H. Dean Rutherford. My dad has been the single greatest influence on my character, my development, my life.

My dad taught me everything: how to live, love, work, preach, and forgive. He's been my #1 encourager, my mentor, my ministry partner, and my best friend. He is truly my hero!

I love you, Dad, and am eternally grateful that our Heavenly Father let me have you as my earthly father.

Your #1 Fan,
David

CONTENTS

The Original G.I. Joe

"Let's go, Joe!" My dirt mounds were set, and my G.I. Joe action-figure, with nineteen individual pivot points, was perfectly positioned for the next backyard adventure. Joe's Five-Star Jeep, complete with trailer *and* spare tire, was camouflaged behind the juniper bush, ready to transport Joe wherever he needed to go—to defend the weak, to stand up for honor and valor, to tackle the next difficult challenge. He was focused, ambitious; he had a plan, man!

Joe could handle anything the world might dish out. Nothing and no one could stop ol' Joe. Except my mom when she called us both in for dinner.

"You'll get 'em tomorrow, Joe!" My childish imagination ran wild, envisioning the challenges Joe would encounter in the morning. Whatever life might throw at him, I was confident he would always do the right thing. But for now, he slept under my pillow, waiting for another day to live life to the fullest.

Actually, my older brothers were the ones who owned

the G.I. Joes. I just borrowed them when they weren't paying attention. They were much older than me and were wrapped up in adventures of their own. They didn't care if I played with them. If baby David stayed out of their way, they were happy. And that was fine with me. Joe didn't need any big brothers messing with his adventures, anyway!

Another Joe caught my attention early in my life. It happened at Sunday school one day when I was about five years old. My teacher brought out the famous flannel board and the box of characters that were going to be part of the day's story. There were all the regular players—the shepherd-looking guys, and animals, of course. And then there was this one new guy...

"Who is *that*?" I leaned in to inspect the boy, who was clothed in the most colorful robe I'd ever seen on a flannel-board figure.

My teacher smiled. "This is Joseph. He has quite a story."

"I bet he *does*! Look at that robe!" I picked up the figure and counted all the many colors. I decided right then that if I were a flannel-board character, I'd wanna be this guy.

"God had a very special plan for Joseph." My teacher took the figure from me and stuck him up on the flannel board. "But his life wasn't easy. In fact, he had to endure difficult challenges for many, many years."

"With a coat like that?"

My teacher laughed. "Well, the coat is what started it all. God was the one who finished it, though. He inspired Joseph all the way and helped him do the right thing, even when life was hard. We'll read all about him in the book of Genesis."

"I can't wait!" I wanted to learn all about this boy with the fancy robe: God-inspired Joe. There was something mesmerizing about him. As I stared into his eyes on the flannel board, I decided that I wanted God to inspire *me* to do the right thing for the rest of my life, too—just like he did for Joseph. This Joseph guy was me, and I was him. Little did I realize just how true that was.

Joseph's Story

The Bible records Joseph's story in Genesis 37 and 39 to 47. Joseph was a shepherd boy, born into a Hebrew family. He had eleven brothers, but his father, Jacob, liked Joseph the best, so he doted on him and treated him better than he treated his other sons. That's how Joseph got the colorful robe.

And boy, did he love it! He wore it everywhere, even to places where a robe like that wouldn't be acceptable attire. You know how spoiled children can act sometimes. "See my new outfit? Yeah, Daddy got it just for me. Isn't it beautiful? I think I'll wear it 24/7."

Yeah, that might have been Joseph.

Joseph also had a couple of dreams that involved his brothers and parents bowing down to him. And he might have bragged about those *a little*, while smoothing his colorful sleeves to show off the splendor of his robe.

And—surprise, surprise—Joe's brothers got jealous. But instead of taping Joe to a flagpole or giving him a swirlie, they beat him, tossed him in a cistern, and sold him to some Ishmaelite traders. And that robe? By the time the brothers were finished with that thing, it wasn't fit to be a dust rag.

Joe's brothers came up with a convincing story to prove to their father that his favorite son was dead. And while Jacob tore his clothes in anguish, refusing to be comforted, the brothers brushed their hands together in satisfaction. "Whew. That's the end of that dreamer!"

Joseph's adventure, however, had just begun. He was taken to Egypt, where he was sold as a slave to the house of Potiphar. Stripped of his coat and his dad's protection and favor, Joseph could have become bitter, but instead, he chose to do his best for his earthly master and for God. Potiphar noticed Joseph's talent, positive attitude, and work ethic, and soon put him in charge of all his affairs. Potiphar's wife noticed Joseph, too—but she had a different sort of affair in mind. When he refused her, she accused him of improper behavior, which earned Joseph a one-way ticket to prison.

Joseph didn't just sit in prison. He worked hard while exhibiting honesty and integrity. This was quickly noticed by the warden, who put Joseph in charge of all the prisoners. Joseph helped a couple of them interpret their dreams—using a gift from God that would place him, two years later, in a position to interpret a dream for Pharaoh. Joseph spoke boldly and truthfully about the dream, and Pharaoh made Joseph his second-in-command.

Because of Joseph's dream interpretations, Egypt began saving food in preparation for a famine. And when the famine hit, who showed up begging for food? Joseph's brothers.

They didn't recognize Joseph—even though he was probably wearing something pretty terrific, being second-in-command—but Joseph sure recognized them. What would he say to his brothers, who had sold him so many years earlier? "Guys, check it out! I got a brand-new, better robe now!" Or, "Hey—I knew you'd come when you ran out of food. I've got some friends down at the jail setting up a room just for you."

No. After giving them some tests to make sure they were no longer the selfish, angry men they had once been, Joseph chose to forgive his brothers—embracing and kissing them, and letting them know that what they had planned for harm, God had used for good in all of their lives.

How could Joseph do that, after all those terrible years as a slave, a prisoner—abandoned and alone for decades on foreign soil?

Joseph was the original G.I. Joe: God-Inspired Joe. He earned his flannel-board fame by living an upright life no matter what, all the while relying on God's plan. He was a survivor, a leader, and a model of strength, honesty, and loyalty during uncertainty and suffering.

My Story and Yours

I can imagine what you're thinking right now: "Brother David, that is some spectacular story. But it happened in another time, another culture. How can you say that you're Joseph and Joseph is you? Were you ever sold as a slave, or put in prison, or placed second-in-command of a kingdom? Are you lost in some G.I. Joe action figure fantasy?"

No, my friend, I'm not (at least, I don't think so). And no, I haven't experienced exactly what Joseph did. But there have been parallels to my own life, which I'll share with you in this book. Why? So you can see that God is able to help you, guide you, and inspire you to make it through all your difficult challenges, while keeping you close to him. He did it for Joseph, and he's doing it for me. Every day.

Did any part in my brief retelling of Joseph's story tug at your heart? Has God given you a dream? Do you live in a dysfunctional family? Have you ever been wrongly accused? Has the uncertainty of life separated you from the people you love the most? Have you been waiting a long time for God to fulfill a promise or answer a prayer? If you can answer yes to any one of these questions, you're going to want to stick with me through this book.

There is hope, friends! The truth is, God has a great purpose for your life. He might not call you to save a nation, but He will call you to make a difference for Him in your family and your workplace, even when things aren't going exactly as you planned. Your life may look a lot like Joseph's—full of hurts, setbacks, and disappointments. Take heart! Your story is not over yet. We, like Joseph, can experience the power of relying on God every step of the way. So, throw on your most colorful robe (or blanket, if you don't do robes), and let's go on a fantastic journey together with God-Inspired Joe.

CHAPTER ONE

Dream-Chaser

The year was 1976. The Boston Celtics and Phoenix Suns were playing each other in game 5 of the NBA finals. The Suns sank a jumper at the buzzer to send the game into the *third* overtime.

The energy in our living room was off the charts. This was no ordinary basketball game! I scanned the room, filled with family and friends and kids from our church youth group. The two most powerful men in my family— my dad and my older brother, Dudley—were rooting for Phoenix. I was a twelve-year-old sports genius at the time, and as baby of the family was looking for a way to move up in my standings. I knew just what to do: I rooted for Boston. It was a bold move, but hey—they won! Boy did that shake things up.

You can imagine the scene, right? Me, a cocky preteen, jumping up and down, yelling out victory chants and pointing at the older, "wiser" sport fans. *"Oh, yeah! Celtics win! Celtics win! I picked the winner!"*

The Boston Celtics have been my team ever since. I

loved John "Hondo" Havlicek and read any book I could get my hands on about him. When Larry Bird came along a few years later, he became my favorite player. Basketball was also my favorite sport to play, and while on the high school team, I picked up the nickname Bird.

And no one ever forgot that glorious moment when all the power in the room had to bow to my sports greatness! (At least, *I've* never forgotten.)

That's about as close as I've ever come to having my brothers and parents bow down to me. And I've sure never had a dream about them doing so. But what if I did?

What if I saw you at church and told you I'd had a couple of dreams that you and your family were bowing down to me? I'm sure you'd slap a knee and laugh out loud. "Whoa, that's a good one, David! What have you been eating before bed?" You might call me "your highness," shake my hand, and then get yourself to a safe place to sort out your new, unflattering opinion of me.

But what if the next day, I showed up at your doorstep and told you that those dreams were glimpses of the future? You'd whip out your phone and call the authorities to pick me up. And then you'd find another church to attend. In a different town.

Joseph's brothers faced a similar dilemma, but it was much more serious. This was their little brother Joseph, Daddy's favorite, doing the dreaming. And in Jacob's family, there were no safe spaces to deal with negative feelings.

Set Up for Failure

To understand Joseph, his brothers, and why the beginning of this story goes down the cistern, so to speak, we need to check out the backstory. Joseph was brought up in a family that, at least in some ways, wasn't so different from many present-day households. He had a father who looked the other way, pretending all would be okay. I can almost hear him mutter, "Boys will be boys," while his sons called the shots.

Joseph's mother, Rachel, had died when he was 10, as she gave birth to his younger brother, Benjamin (Genesis 35:16–21). Her absence, combined with Jacob's passivity and the brothers' rage and jealousy, created a space for sin to creep in.

Joseph's brothers took every opportunity to give him a tough time. To be honest, that's part of an older brother's job description. I have two older brothers who claim they *love* me, yet I barely survived! I can't imagine having ten older brothers, all doing their best to make life miserable.

Yet, in the midst of this chaos, Joseph had a dream. Despite all the dysfunction, Joseph knew God had a purpose for him, so he clung to that hope and refused to let go.

The Power of Joe's Dreams

People are always trying to analyze dreams. There's the one where you show up for a test, but you haven't attended class all semester. Or that one where you forget your locker combination. And that one when you show up for a meeting and you're naked—horrors! What do these dreams mean? Is our subconscious trying to tell us something? Do these dreams have any power over our life, besides causing us to make sure we're dressed before stepping out the door? Not really.

Except prophetic dreams. Those are the ones you know are from God. They have staying power. And Joseph had *two*.

> One night, Joseph had a dream, and when he told his brothers about it, they hated him more than ever. "Listen to this dream," he said. "We were out in the field, tying up bundles of grain. Suddenly my bundle stood up, and your bundles all gathered around and bowed low before mine!"
> —**Genesis 37:5–7** *(NLT)*

Can you imagine the joy around the house after that conversation? But wait, there's more.

> Soon Joseph had another dream, and again he told his brothers about it. "Listen, I have had another dream," he said. "The sun, moon, and eleven stars bowed low before me!"
> —**Genesis 37:9** *(NLT)*

This dream was so upsetting to the family that it brought a rare scolding from Jacob. And while that made the brothers happy, their jealousy grew, and their hatred for Joseph darkened their hearts.

But Joseph knew his dreams were from God, and that gave his life power and purpose. It's the only way he could have survived the mistreatment by his brothers and the lonely years in Egypt. Knowing he had a mission and a destiny helped Joseph remain steady. He was propelled into the work of God through this conviction that God was at work in and through him. He was committed to excellence and loyalty no matter what.

Excellence Through the Struggle

Think about the moment Joseph's life changed. One day, he was the favored son; the next, he was on his way to an uncertain future in Egypt. This would kill most people's motivation to fulfill their dreams. But not Joseph. He had the attitude of *whatever*—as in, "whatever it takes to make this dream become reality, I'll do it." Whether he was taking care of the entire household of Potiphar or attending to the needs of prisoners, Joseph did it all with excellence.

We live in a culture today where excellence is overrated. If you do things too well, people may suspect you of being slick or fake. If we work too hard at our jobs, we're labeled a goodie-two-shoes or accused of trying to impress the boss. Mediocrity is revered today. Authenticity—that's what really matters, we're told!

But when you meet the Lord face to face, would you rather have Him say, "Well done, good and faithful servant," or "You stunk, but at least you were you"? Joseph was able to be excellent *and* authentic because he knew who he was and what God had called him to be. He wasn't idly thinking about his destiny without doing anything about it. He pressed on, even when the odds were against him.

There was another moment, decades later, when Joseph's life changed again. One day he was a prisoner, and the next, he was second-in-command behind Pharaoh! In that elevated position, Joseph had power to effect change and fulfill his dream.

Do you want to pursue excellence and succeed? Some people spend a lot of money trying to uncover the secret of success. But the secret is, *there's no secret*. Stepping into what God has for us is hard work! It takes commitment and faith. There's nothing mystical about it. It's not a matter of praying the right prayer or saying the right things. It's not naming it and claiming it. It's a day-in, day-out pursuit of God. It's about taking hold of the situation, even when it's not what you want, and asking for God's help every single moment of your life. It's about asking for direction, asking for blessing, and committing yourself to excellence.

Loyalty Despite Letdowns

No matter what was done to him, Joseph never cast people aside. They were an important part of his dreams.

Jacob's favoritism toward Joseph caused a huge family rift, yet Joseph never held it against him. After Joe's brothers beat, brutalized, robbed, and sold him to the Ishmaelites, Joseph refused to enact vengeance when given the chance. Instead, he embraced his brothers and wept tears of joy (Genesis 45:14–15).

Joseph served Potiphar, his master, loyally, even

though it got him thrown in jail when he refused the advances of Potiphar's wife (Genesis 39:2–20). He helped those in the jail loyally, putting their needs ahead of his own (Genesis 39:21–23).

And Joseph served Pharaoh and all of Egypt, loyally and efficiently, even though the leader and the nation represented nothing but pain and isolation for him (Genesis 41).

Joseph's dreams caused him to see the *bigger* picture. They inspired him to love those who were cruel to him. They enabled him to forgive. Joseph blessed every person he could because he believed people were in his life by divine appointment.

Dream Big

As a preteen, my dreams consisted of becoming a professional athlete, hanging out with girls, and eating Mexican food. Not prophetic at all! (Though I have consumed my share of chips and guacamole.) In Bible college, my dreams changed. As a young man, a little older than 17, I began to understand what God wanted for me. Some of this direction came through the Word of God. Other times, I found it through God's people.

One day when I was in Bible college, my brother Dudley called and asked me this question: "David, what are you doing?" Well, I was playing basketball, studying, dating girls, and eating Mexican food! What he meant was, "What are you doing in ministry? How has God wired you? What are you doing with that?" That made me put down the chips and guac and start thinking a little deeper.

I began to look for opportunities to try out my gifts.

And one day, at age 18, I was tricked into being a guest preacher at a little church in Arcola, Missouri. I did my best to prepare a ripped-off sermon from my dad, titled "Stop the Sermon" (clever title, right?). I prayed and gave the congregation my best effort—and something profound happened to me that morning. Before I was finished preaching, I knew it was what God had gifted me to do. Ever since that day, God has not allowed me to "stop the sermon"! In fact, here I am, thirty-eight years later, in my office, preparing a sermon for this weekend.

The dream established in my heart that day in Missouri didn't always make sense. There were bumps, detours, doubts, and many struggles along the way. Lots of schooling and study and hard work comes with being a preacher. But when I look back on the journey, I can tell you, God has been faithful, and it's a great feeling to know I was always right where He wanted me to be.

I want that feeling for you, too, so let's get personal for a moment. What do you believe God is calling you to? What dream has He given you? Think about that calling—draw a circle around it—and step inside.

Now, hold up the life of Joseph and compare it with your own. Specifically, compare those God-inspired character traits of faith, excellence, and loyalty:

How straight and tall is your life as a spiritual leader compared to his?

Where are you lacking, and where are you excelling?

Are you committed to excellence and to prayer?

Maybe today would be a good time to revisit a failed dream or to reevaluate past dreams. Maybe now is the time to consider how God may use you in the lives of other people. Think about your role as a parent, a sibling, a co-worker. When was the last time you sat down and told somebody about Jesus? When was the last time you gave without expecting anything in return?

Finding your dream and pursuing it with excellence is crucial to seeing God move in your life. But just like Joseph, you also need to be people-focused. People don't gain favor with God by trampling over others. They gain favor by having a loving, forgiving spirit and attitude.

Ask yourself: Are relationships disposable to you, or are you loyal? When things go bad, do you burn bridges, cut ties, and ignore those who you feel have wronged you? Or do you embrace them with open arms, pouring blessing upon them even when the world would say they don't deserve it?

The Apostle Paul wrote, "If it is possible, as far as it depends on you, live at peace with everyone" (Romans 12:18). Peter also preached to "seek peace and pursue it" (1 Peter 3:11, quoting Psalm 34:14). The word he used for *pursue* is the same root as *persecute*—to go after it with energy![1]

Do everything you can to make your relationships the best they can be. You can seek peace even when past hurts still linger. Imagine how different things would be if you gave yourself to prayer, to working hard, and to treating people as though God sent them to you. Live in these principles so that you can be a better leader and example of Christ.

WORKBOOK

Chapter One Questions

Question: What are some difficult dynamics in your current family and/or your family of origin? How have these dynamics shaped your decisions and dreams, for good or for bad? How can you overcome (and even use) the difficulties of your family dynamics to fulfill God's purposes for you?

Question: Are you committed to pursuing excellence, or do you do just enough to get by? What are some specific ways you can "up your game" in your various roles at home, work, and church, and in pursuing your God-given dreams?

Question: What is the difference between loyalty and enabling? How can you be loyal to the people God has put in your life while still challenging them to be and do their best? How can you support others in their dreams, even if their success eclipses yours?

Action: Take time to dream. Then write in a journal or jot down ideas in a notebook. How would you describe the dream(s) that God has put in your heart? Will your dreams build others up and show Christ to them, or are they all about you? Ask God to continually reveal and clarify a God-sized vision in your heart of how He can use you to help others for His glory.

CHAPTER TWO

Speed Bumps

There I was, cruising the streets, trying to spot my friend Merle's house, when *bam!* My whole car came off the ground, jolting me to attention. The car began to bounce as it threatened to careen off the road. My mind went to worst-case scenarios. But before I knew it, I was back on track, tires firmly gripping the pavement.

I had hit a speed bump while going forty miles an hour. But not just any speed bump: it was the biggest speed bump you'd ever see in your life, I guarantee. And though I didn't lose control of the car, I'm almost certain I lost control of my state of mind. "It's a *miracle* I survived!" was my dramatic response. Poor Merle—I've never been to his house since.

Speed bumps slow you down. They're the not-too-pleasant reminders you need to pay attention, keep your eyes on the road, and stay focused on what matters. Just as I'm convinced God has a plan for your life, I know there are times when He slows you down, jolts you awake, and forces you to pay attention to what's going on around you so you can learn the lessons He's trying to teach you.

Maybe He wants to address your attitude or your desires. Maybe He wants to show His power or remind you that He's with you. Whatever His reasoning—and I promise, He *always* has a reason—speed bumps are part of the Christian journey.

The biggest speed bump of my life came when my dad was let go from his senior pastor position at his church. It was Valentine's Day, and I was in ninth grade. My mom picked me up from school to tell me the news. What a shock! I had been born and raised in the same town and had only attended that one church. I was a happy little runt who knew nothing else. All the older kids in my family were out on their own by this time, so it was just me, my dad, and my mom, packing up our belongings and heading out of our comfortable little town toward a very uncertain future.

I'll never forget stopping for dinner in Oklahoma City on the way between Kansas and Florida. My dad broke down and wept. I had never seen my dad break down— ever! Nobody ate much of that meal. I took comfort, at least, that we were in the crisis *together*. My ninth-grade heart was convinced that no matter where we went and what my dad ended up doing for a job, we'd support each other and come out of this tough situation just fine.

But we were about to be separated. Did I mention that this was a *big* speed bump?

Slow Down, Joe!

God used speed bumps throughout Joseph's life to develop his character and keep him focused on what mattered. It took a lifetime of these speed bumps for God to form Joe into the great, compassionate, wise leader that he became. As you can imagine, however, a lifetime of hitting those bumps could knock a few things loose! And in Joseph's case, there might have been a *couple* of things that needed to go from his character.

Criticism, Conceit, and Self-Centeredness

Remember when you were a kid and brought home your report card? Did your teacher ever write in the dreaded comment section? "Davey is a charming boy, but he needs to focus more on his schoolwork and less on telling jokes." Or, "Jenny is an excellent student but needs to work on getting along better with her classmates." Ouch. The comment section was there because sometimes the grade didn't tell the whole story.

When we first meet Joseph in Genesis 37, he's a competent young man—able to tend his father's flocks and work for his half-brothers and his father's wives. He would get all A's on his first-quarter shepherd's report card. But we read this:

Joseph, a young man of seventeen, was tending the flocks with his brothers, the sons of Bilhah and the sons of Zilpah, his father's wives, and he brought their father a bad report about them.

—Genesis 37:2

Joseph would get an A in another subject: observation! He sounds like a real quality-control type, but he used this talent unwisely. A teacher might have written, "While Joseph is detail-oriented and driven, he needs to mind his own business once in a while instead of being critical of others."

Yes. Mm-hmm—see how that comment section brings out the whole truth? Joseph was a bit over-critical. In this passage, he comes across as a spoiled, immature brat saying, "I'm going to tell Daddy on you." The Hebrew phrase for bringing a "bad report" means to slander.[2] In other words, Joe reported his brothers to Dad *with the intent of bringing them down.*

I think we all know someone like this, and if you're honest, you've had moments when *you* fit the bill, too. I can think of plenty of times when I've reveled in uncovering someone's faults or missteps. There have been times when I've focused only on the negative, especially when it comes to others. I've used words to tear down and not build up. I've been like Joe.

Seeing faults in others does not mean you have to declare them or bring them to the surface. The old saying, "If you've got nothing good to say, then don't say anything at all," rings true. First Corinthians 13:5 observes that love "keeps no record of wrongs." Instead, love builds up. It acknowledges that everyone has faults but that it does no one any good to sit there and keep pointing them out.

Joseph's report, though it may have been accurate, annoyed his brothers. It revealed that he had been watching them, making a list of faults and weaknesses. He lost their respect because of his critical attitude. It would take a very big speed bump to jar that loose from his character. Joseph also saw himself as being more important than his brothers. How could this happen? Genesis 37:3 explains that Jacob "loved Joseph more than any of his other sons ... and he made a richly ornamented robe for him." Wow. Think about that for a moment. The Bible clearly says Jacob loved Joseph more than the others, violating every principle of parenting! It was favoritism, plain and simple. It's like if I were the commissioner of the NBA but wore a Boston Celtics jersey (obviously, the only right choice) everywhere I went. That was Jacob's approach to parenting.

The ceremonial robe was supposed to be for special occasions, but Joseph wore it everywhere, so it served as a constant reminder to everyone of his place within his father's heart. But more than that, the robe carried the rights of inheritance. In other words, Jacob was making it clear that Joseph, who was not the oldest son, was the primary heir. This dysfunction goes way back to when Jacob grabbed the birthright from his older brother, Esau. No wonder he didn't think twice about passing over his oldest son in favor of Joseph![3]

It's no surprise that the brothers hated Joseph for all the things the robe represented. Meanwhile, Joseph lived with a spirit of "Look at me! I'm the one!" I think of an Olympic champion wearing his medals all the time, showing off the reward to which only he has access. A teacher may have written in his comment section: "Joseph is a privileged young man but would do well to consider others' feelings and not brag so much."

Having medals doesn't mean you have to wear them, and great opportunities don't always have to be flaunted in front of everyone you know. Today's culture teaches us we need to promote ourselves if we're going to get to the top. Scroll a little through your favorite social media sites and you'll see everyone's grand accomplishments. I have a good friend who calls Facebook "Bragbook." Supposedly, you need to hustle and push your own agenda. But the Bible teaches the opposite. "Humble yourselves, therefore, under God's mighty hand, that he may lift you up in due time" (1 Peter 5:6).

Yet there was Joseph, strutting around in his beautiful robe and making sure everyone knew about his bright future. I can just imagine God's comment section on this young man's report card: "Joseph's going to be a great leader one day, but it's not going to happen the way he thinks it will. His pride needs to go. His critical attitude needs to go. And there will be a pit and a prison way before there'll ever be a palace."

I'm sure there are times when God would write the same about us: "I plan to bless him, but he's not ready to receive yet."

A critical spirit and a conceited attitude will always produce a person with a self-centered focus. Genesis 37:5 says that "Joseph had a dream, and when he told it to his brothers, they hated him all the more." Joseph believed that his dreams were from God, so the problem wasn't the dreams, but the fact that he felt obligated to tell his brothers about them.

Like most seventeen-year-olds, Joseph made everything all about him—what he felt, what he wanted, what his future held. He wanted to be the highlight of the conversation, and he wanted his brothers to know just how great he had it.

Many of us struggle with a need for the spotlight. You hear from kindergarten on that you're clever, wonderful, and smart. Most teenagers today have had every golden moment of their life filtered and chronicled on social media. If they don't get a reality check, they'll become critical, conceited, and self-centered adults!

There comes a time when you need to exhibit wisdom, stop glorifying yourself, and keep your mouth shut for the good of others. Proverbs 13:3 says, "Those who guard their lips preserve their lives, but those who speak rashly will come to ruin." A wise way to handle the spotlight is to take the Proverbs 27:2 approach: "Let someone else praise you, and not your own mouth; an outsider, and not your own lips." If you want to be a servant of Jesus Christ, you need to stop glorifying yourself and allow Him to reign over you. Not everyone wants the play-by-play of your dreams.

About That Big Speed-Bump...

My dad got a new job working at a boys' ranch in Orlando, Florida. We spent the summer there, living in a small, run-down trailer, getting used to the new "normal." But I was about to start my first year in high school (tenth grade at that time), and that wasn't anywhere near the boys' camp. So it was off to Tampa, Florida, for me, to

stay with an elder's family, while my mom and dad remained at the camp.

My parents moved into town a few months later, but
the beginning of that year was horrible for me. I was
lonely as a new student at a huge high school. I remember
walking the hallways, seeing kids who looked like the
kids I knew back in Kansas, but I didn't know anyone.
And no one knew me, either. I tried talking to people
(mostly girls), but I was met with icy stares. I was isolated
from everything comfortable, and I fought feelings of being cast out—from my town, from my church, and even
from my own family. I had moments when I blamed my
dad for losing his job in Wichita, and there were times
when I blamed the people who were instrumental in letting him go. Didn't anyone realize their actions would
have painful consequences for me, a kid? Didn't they
care?

Looking back now, I realize that God allowed this
speed bump in my life to shake loose my critical spirit,
conceited attitude, and self-focus. In fact, I honestly believe now that if I hadn't left Kansas, I might have died.
Why do I think that? I was the baby of the family, and we
all know parents are a little looser with the discipline by
the time the baby comes along. I had my run of Wichita,
Kansas. I rode my bike wherever I wanted, when I wanted.
No one kept tabs on me. One New Year's Eve, when my
parents were at a ministry function, I sat home all by myself and ate nothing but Doritos and ranch dip all night
long.

I wasn't a bad kid. I loved God, and I never *planned* to
get in trouble. But I shudder to think what I might have

gotten talked into as a teenager in that town—with a car and friends who might have introduced me to worse vices than ranch dip. God needed me out of there so I could focus my life on something more than having a good time.

During my stay in Tampa, God humbled me. He removed the self-focus from my heart. And with that gone, He was able to get my heart ready for a new dream and a desire: to serve Him in ministry and do everything I could to bring my family back together.

Watch Out for That...

Friends, there are speed bumps everywhere. You watch for them in parking lots and in neighborhoods, and though you hate them, you navigate them, right? You realize they are there for your protection and the protection of others.

Your life speed-bumps work the same way. You can't avoid them—God would not want you to avoid them—so how best can you navigate them? Have you hit a speed bump lately? What do you think God is trying to knock loose from your character?

WORKBOOK

Chapter Two Questions

Question: What are some "speed bumps" in your life that God has used to slow you down and help develop your character? How have you reacted to these challenges?

Question: How could Joseph have dealt with his brothers' misdeeds in a way that would have been gracious and redemptive instead of slanderous? What does Matthew 18:15–17 teach about the way a Christian should respond to another's sin? In what type of situations should you follow these guidelines, and in what type of situations should you overlook an offense (see Proverbs 19:11)?

Question: What are some areas where you tend to view yourself as better than others—more talented, more popular, more spiritual, or more important? What does it mean to "humble yourself," and how can you do that on a practical level?

Action: The best way to change a self-centered focus is to start focusing instead on God and others. List five ways you can stay focused on God and five ways you can start focusing on others. Then choose at least one action from each list to begin implementing this week.

CHAPTER THREE

Hold Tight

In 1970, the makers of G.I. Joe came up with a new, fascinating feature for their action-figure: Kung-Fu grip. The commercial described it this way: "G.I. Joe has hands that grip! Fingers you hold open and then close. Hands that hold on with a Kung-Fu grip. The grip that you help Joe use in self-defense!"[4] Whoever invented that feature had a real understanding of life. Sometimes we are hit with a situation that is so tough, it knocks us for a loop, and all we can do is hold on tight for survival.

Function Out of Dysfunction

God-Inspired Joe had plenty of opportunities to use his kung-fu grip. Genesis 37:18–36 details his brothers' attack and the casual way they discussed his demise over a meal! I wonder if Joseph could hear them talking. Did he believe he was going to die right then?

His brother Judah came to the rescue, sort of. "Come, let's sell him to the Ishmaelites and not lay our hands on

him; after all, he is our brother, our own flesh and blood"
(Genesis 37:26–27).

I can imagine Joseph, down there at the bottom of the
cistern, letting out a sad sigh. "Thanks, Judah. Buy yourself something nice with the money you get for me." The
dysfunction in Joseph's family had finally erupted into a
violent and hateful event, and Joseph took the fall. But Joseph never retaliated.

It's interesting to note that scholars refer to Joseph as
the Jesus of the Old Testament. If you follow the rest of
Joseph's story carefully, you will see there is no real flaw
in him—no flagrant sin. You might think that Joseph, of
all people, would have an excuse to live his life as a negative, resentful, vengeful person. Yet Joseph kept getting
better. He was a survivor, and he didn't survive by
fighting with others, clawing his way to the top. Instead,
everywhere he went, he used the tools of kindness and
honesty to hold tight to God during all of his trials.

Tools for the Tested

It's nice to see kindness making a comeback in our culture. Memes, T-shirts, coffee mugs—visual reminders to
be kind are everywhere. Sounds easy, right? If everyone
would just do it, *that* would be something. Yet even in this
culture of "be kind" sentiments, what we often experience
is hatred.

Hatred is like a dirty bomb—there's a big explosion,
but that's not the end of it. It lingers, festers, and taints
everything in its path. Just follow the comment trail after
a hateful rant on social media and you'll see what I mean.

The hurt goes on and on.

I believe that after Joseph's brothers sold him, they were haunted daily by what they had done. Every moment spent with their father must have brought them guilt and shame. I wonder how they were able to keep that terrible secret for so long. It must have eaten away at them, weakened them, even affected their health. Their suffering may have been even greater than Joseph's during those decades they were separated. That's how hatred works.

Unlike his brothers, Joseph saw the need for kindness in his family, and he extended it to them as soon as he was able. As Ephesians 4:32 says, "Be kind and compassionate to one another, forgiving each other, just as in Christ God forgave you."

God calls us to be kind (1 Corinthians 13:4), and it's always good practice to start with our own family members. Love within a family can keep that family together even when circumstances threaten to tear it apart.

Wouldn't it be great if honesty would make a comeback? Unfortunately, we live in a world of deceit these days. If you don't believe me, try to find a news agency you can trust to give you unbiased information. Fake news—who would have thought that would be a thing? Yet deceit and deception were already around back in Joseph's day.

It's interesting, but Joseph's brothers didn't come right out and lie to Jacob. They didn't *tell* him that Joseph was dead. Instead, they deceived him into coming to that conclusion on his own (Genesis 37:31–33). It's not surprising the sons were this way since Jacob was one of the greatest deceivers of all time. If ESPN had a Top 20 for biblical masters of deception, Jacob would easily make the list. Even his name pointed to this problem: Jacob means "heel grabber."[5] All throughout his life, Jacob grabbed whatever he could get his hands on, no matter whom he had to manipulate along the way.

Galatians 6:7 tells us, "God cannot be mocked. A man reaps what he sows." If you live a life of deceit, you will reap a crop of lies. Joseph chose to live a life of honesty instead of deceit. He was truthful with Potiphar, with Potiphar's wife, with the men in the jail, and with Pharaoh.

All of us are prone to give in to lies, deceit, and manipulation. The world gives us excuses to rationalize: "Look at all you've been through. One little lie won't hurt." But it does. It can set the tone for a whole family, be passed down through generations, and come back to hurt the one who started it all. Joseph broke his family's cycle of lies with honesty.

Look Up

When he was thrown into that cistern, Joseph likely hit the stone that prevented the water from draining away. Literally, he hit rock bottom. But when you are at rock bottom, the only place you can go is up.

We're all going to hit rock bottom at some point in our lives; this is true even of God's children. The key is where you place your focus and how you respond. Do pits of worry, ill health, poor finances, professional droughts, or significant loss cause you to go to a dark place of anguish and turmoil? Do you lash out at others? Or do you lie, doing whatever it takes to get you out of trouble?

God has a plan—*no matter what*. Keep your eyes on Him and remember that kindness and honesty are building blocks for a strong character that will help you hold tight during life's hardships.

Truths for the Tested

You may be shaking your head at this point, saying, "Brother David, I am in a *horrible* pit right now. This holding on thing is hard to do. I'm doing my best to be kind and honest, but my hands are slipping. I need more than Kung-Fu grip!"

Fun fact: the makers of G.I. Joe discovered the same thing. While the concept was wonderful, the drawback was the rubber material used. After an extended amount of play, the rubber proved to be fragile,[6] causing Joe to lose his grip.

Can you imagine the panic when the toy developers discovered this problem? "We're getting reports that G.I. Joes are falling out of trees and off of cliffs! What's going on? He's supposed to have Kung-Fu grip, people! The kids of the world are counting on us. Somebody fix this— now." I picture toy execs scurrying through the hallways yelling, *"Redesign, redesign, redesign!"*

Thankfully, the grip that God gives you to hang on during tough times is perfectly planned for you. *His* design is trustworthy.

So while you are holding on, wrap your hands around these truths:

1. There's no panic in heaven, only plans. Think about

Joseph in his richly colored coat, strutting around like some movie star prepared to collect his Oscar. Then, out of nowhere, his brothers ripped off the coat and threw him into a pit. He was cold, naked, bruised, sore, bleeding, and scared.

The God of the universe notices when a sparrow falls to the ground (Matthew 10:25), so He certainly noticed and cared about Joseph. But there was no panic in heaven. God didn't say, "Uh oh." He wasn't surprised or startled. He saw the whole picture and knew this was an important step in Joseph's journey.

If you find yourself in a pit today and want to throw your hands up, weep, worry, and fret, God says, "Don't do it. I'm in charge. This is a time of testing for you. Trust Me."

> *Consider it pure joy, my brothers [and sisters], whenever you face trials of many kinds, because you know that the testing of your faith develops perseverance. Perseverance must finish its work so that you may be mature and complete, not lacking anything.*
> *—James 1:2-4*

I wish we could grow in perseverance when things are going well, but it doesn't work that way. Most people would rather skip right over a trial if they could. Or at least, we'd prefer our life tests be like the tests we took in school, where we learn and study first and *then* take the big test. But God flips that around: test first, lesson second. There are also times when He'll send a second test to see if the lesson stuck!

The good news is that God's tests are always True/False, and there is only one question: "In the toughest, most difficult times of your life, you can totally trust God. True or false?" That's it. When circumstances are stacked against you, that's the only test that matters.

2. The word "coincidence" is not in God's vocabulary. You may chalk good things up to coincidence or luck, but there's no happenstance with God. Everything is either from Him or permitted by Him. It's called blessing!

Despite all the bad in Joseph's life, God came through with some big blessings. It "just so happened" that a caravan of traders passed by at the exact time Joseph's brothers were plotting to leave him for dead (Genesis 37:25–26). Then, he "just happened" to work for a guy whose wife found him attractive, and "just happened" to be thrown in jail, where he "just happened" to interpret a dream for a prisoner who "just happened" to work for Pharaoh, who had a dream that needed an interpretation—something right up Joe's alley (Genesis 41:14–15)! Finally, it "just happened" that his brothers came to Egypt, placing Joseph in a position to heal the past and restore his family (Genesis 45:5).

You can't see the whole plan, but God can. He works everything out for the good. Your life is like a ten-thousand-piece jigsaw puzzle. You hold one piece in your hand and wonder what it's going to look like when God's finished with you. Joseph being in a pit was one piece of the puzzle. Being sold to the slave traders was another piece. Being sold to Potiphar, interpreting dreams, the famine in the land—piece by piece, the picture formed. Joseph may have had moments when he questioned what the result would be, but he never stopped trusting.

Romans 8:29 says God wants you to be "conformed to the likeness of his Son." He wants you to take on the nature and personality of Jesus Christ. And not just when it comes to trusting! He also wants you to have the fruit of the Spirit: "love, joy, peace, patience, kindness, goodness, faithfulness, gentleness and self-control" (Galatians 5:22–23).

3. Your deliverance is on the way, but it may be disguised as more trouble. Think again about Joseph in the pit. He was having the worst day of his life when suddenly, his brothers pulled him out. Time to celebrate, right? Wrong. Just when Joseph thought he was going to get an apology, he was bound hand-and-foot, tied to a camel, and sold to a bunch of strangers. At this point, he might have screamed, "Please, throw me back in the cistern!"

Things were going to get worse for Joseph. Yet all the while, I can hear God saying, "I'm delivering you. What you think is your greatest struggle is actually the very place I've prepared to make you the successful leader I know you can be!"

In Genesis 45:5, Joseph tells his brothers, "Do not be distressed and do not be angry with yourselves for selling me here [into slavery in Egypt], because it was to save lives that God sent me ahead of you." At that moment, Joseph saw the whole picture. It wasn't his brothers but God who had arranged his journey. It was all part of His plan.

Sometimes you may look around and think that God is nowhere to be found. Every day seems worse than the last. But in those worst moments, God is preparing deliverance. He sees the full picture. He knows how to rescue you, and He knows how to use you. Maybe you're in the pit of loneliness. Maybe you have some habit that needs to be broken. Maybe you're in a pit of sin. It may be the worst feeling in the world right now, but God can and will make a change. You simply must let Him.

Meanwhile, in Tampa...

I continued to walk the dark and unfriendly halls day after day at my new high school, longing for home and family. Wishing I were anywhere but where I was—where hardly anyone would talk to me. I began to lose hope that anything would change.

Then, one day, someone acknowledged my existence! It was at basketball tryouts, when they found out I could bounce a ball and throw it cleanly through the hoop.

"What's your name? Rutherford? Want to join our JV basketball team?"

I smiled for the first time in months. "Sure thing, Coach!" I dribbled the ball, then spun it around on my finger. "And, you know what? You can call me Bird."

As I lifted the ball in the air and sent it flying in for a swish, I could almost see new light and hope shining through that hoop. I didn't know what the distant future held, but at least God was giving me the next piece of the puzzle. And that was something I could hold on to.

WORKBOOK

Chapter Three Questions

Question: Describe the kindest person you have known. How did their kindness shine despite—or because of—the adversity that they faced? Who is someone who needs your kindness today?

Question: What are some ways you see dishonesty and deception in "small ways"—at work, on social media, in relationships, or by political or spiritual leaders? What might be the cost for choosing a life of uncompromising honesty? What will be the rewards?

Question: Have you experienced a "rock bottom" moment? How did it make you stronger than before? How did you learn to trust God through the pain and uncertainty?

Action: Read Psalm 105. What does this psalm reveal about Joseph and his piece in a much bigger puzzle of God's plan for the nation of Israel? How did Joseph's faithfulness position him to be used in God's divine plan? What are some other examples from the Bible, history, your friends' lives, or your life of how faithfulness through a rock-bottom experience works to fulfill God's much bigger plan?

CHAPTER FOUR

Run, Joe, Run!

Sometimes testing comes in the form of temptation, in which case, *don't* hold on.

When they arrived in Egypt, the Ishmaelite traders sold our friend Joe to the house of Potiphar, the captain of the guard for Pharaoh, the king of Egypt. It didn't take long for Potiphar to recognize Joe's intelligence and leadership ability. He also noticed something else: "Potiphar ... realized that the LORD was with Joseph, giving him success in everything he did" (Genesis 39:3 NLT). Potiphar moved Joseph into the main house to oversee his personal and business affairs (Genesis 39:2–4). This was the biggest promotion a slave could hope for!

The only problem for Joe was that being in the big house brought another speed bump: Potiphar's wife.

The Bible says, "Joseph was a very handsome and well-built young man, and Potiphar's wife soon began to look at him lustfully. 'Come and sleep with me,' she demanded" (Genesis 39:6–7 NLT).

This didn't happen just once. The Bible says she put

pressure on Joseph day after day. She must have made it impossible for him to concentrate on his work! At this time, Joseph was a twenty-seven-year-old bachelor, living in a culture that promoted much more sexual freedom than his traditional Hebrew upbringing. I'm sure giving in to the temptation crossed his mind. She was a powerful woman, and he was a slave. He was alone in a foreign country. He had so many reasons to say yes.

Instead, he refused. He clung to his convictions and did what was right. But she kept coming after him, and finally one day, she grabbed him! Joseph tore himself away and ran from the house, leaving his cloak in her hands. Angry and embarrassed at being refused, Potiphar's wife lied about Joseph, claiming he tried to force himself on her (Genesis 39:13–18).

The Bible says that Potiphar's anger burned—but I like to think that his anger burned against his wife for causing him to lose such a valuable house manager (Genesis 39:19). Such an accusation, if taken seriously, would usually lead to death for the perpetrator. (In fact, as Pharaoh's captain of the guard, Potiphar was probably his chief executioner as well.) All things considered, Joseph ending up in jail was like a slap on the wrist. It's as if Potiphar knew his wife had a weakness for handsome young men and a habit of telling stories.

Question from a Five-Year-Old

When I was five years old, I asked my dad this question: "Why are beer commercials the best commercials on TV?" (I was an observant little kid!) My dad told me it was because the beer companies had the most money, so they could afford to hire top-notch writers and directors to produce the best-looking environment for their product. And boy, was he right! They must be creative to tell a story that is so far from reality. They've got horses kicking footballs, footage of the waterfalls where they supposedly collect all of their pure, mountain water, and girls handing out frosty bottles at sunset on every beach. My favorite commercial was one where an ice-cold beer train arrives on a scorching day on a rooftop in New York City. What an awesome party! A person could drink beer all day up there.

And there lies the problem. Getting drunk is outside of God's boundaries—but it sure does look good! Satan is a master at disguising sin as something attractive. He's clever that way. Would anyone try something harmful if they could see and feel the consequences of their decision up front?

Another commercial I thought was funny was one with the Marlboro man, up on top of a mountain on his horse, breathing all that clean air while smoking a cigarette. *What?* And then there were the commercials featuring the tagline, "What happens in Vegas stays in Vegas." Well, that's a big lie.

Joseph knew that "what happens in Egypt doesn't stay in Egypt." He didn't fall for the deception. He knew his God-given dream did not go down an adulterous path, so he hit the road!

Reasons to Run

These days, we are not seeing stampedes of people running from sexual temptation. Almost weekly, there's a breaking story of a sports star, a politician, a high-profile pastor, or some other celebrity failing to stay within proper boundaries. We are saddened as we watch them lose their reputation, career, and family.

The Bible also gives us examples of men who were followers of God yet stumbled in this area. Think about this: the strongest man in the world, Samson, couldn't resist Delilah. The wisest man, Solomon, couldn't resist—well, any woman. And even the most spiritual man, King David, struggled and fell prey to his sexual desires, bringing pain and consequences to the lives of many.

Considering all these examples, you may ask, "Is staying pure these days even possible?" Well, Joseph did it, so let's look at more of his story. How was God-Inspired Joe able to stand up under temptation, in the face of extraordinary pressure?

Genesis 39:8 says "he refused." He didn't skirt the issue. He didn't laugh off Mrs. Potiphar's requests. He simply said no. And then he did it again and again and again.

Along with saying no, Joe gave Potiphar's wife two reasons why he was rejecting her advances.

First, he didn't want to be unfair to his master, who had been good to him (Genesis 39:8). What a principle for us! Giving in to temptation is so often a selfish action. But when we stop and think about others who may be hurt—spouse, kids, parents, friends—it can really put things in perspective.

Second, he didn't want to be disloyal to God (Genesis 39:9). Remember how Pharaoh noticed that the Lord was with Joseph? People don't notice that about a person unless they radiate God's character. It's clear that Joseph was living his life fully for the Lord, and there was no way he was going to let a temporary fling with the boss's wife mess that up.

Are You Ready to Run?

You may be thinking, "I've got this. I know what the Bible says about sexual purity, and I don't see this ever being a problem for me. Bring on the Mrs. (or Mr.) Potiphars!"

Hold up, my friend. Check out 1 Corinthians 10:12: "If you think you are standing strong, be careful not to fall" (NLT).

When I was new in ministry, other pastors warned me, "Women will be drawn to you, and they will come after you. Be careful. Set boundaries." After I had a good belly laugh, I assured my concerned pastor friends I'd be fine. And indeed, nothing happened for a while.

Then, one day, a woman walked into my office and started talking crazy stuff. Clearly, I had been naïve and had underestimated the enemy. I kicked the woman out (I didn't run, because it was *my* office), set counseling guidelines, and placed safeguards around me. One of those safeguards has been my trusted assistant Charlotte, whose office is located between mine and the world. You must get through Charlotte to get to me! And if your name is Mrs. Potiphar, sorry, but you're not getting an appointment.

Do you want to be like God-Inspired Joe and live your life fully for God? Then it will be necessary for you to plan in advance to stand against temptation. I realize that this may be an unpopular topic. There appear to be no boundaries these days when it comes to satisfying sexual appetites. Most young people have seen nothing but sexual promiscuity promoted in their families, on TV, and on social media. We live in a world that trivializes it all. No big deal. Just do what you want.

But God instructs His people to live pure lives. So, if that's you, and you want to be "ready to run," here are some helpful principles to remember:

1. God's standards of right and wrong are unchangeable. It didn't matter how far Joseph was removed from his home, how immoral the culture, how unsettled he felt—God's Word was not altered.

Some people suggest God's standards of morality fluctuate according to the culture, but Jesus Christ said, "Heaven and earth will pass away, but my words will never pass away" (Matthew 24:35).

God's standard doesn't change. It is constant and timeless. No matter what culture says, no matter what well-intentioned people say, God's Word is the same yesterday, today, and forever (Hebrews 13:8).

These days, it feels like the entire world is shifting in one direction while God's Word points us in another. You're faced with a choice. Do you give in and go with the world? It would certainly be easier! Or do you hold true to what His Word says?

Betting on the world is like trying to pick one athlete or team to win the championship. If you're a sports fan, you know how hard that is! There are so many factors you can't see. You don't know what training has been like or if the players are well-rested. You don't know if their diet is on point or if they're going through personal issues to distract them. There is very little you know about the teams and athletes that you support, and that's why most of the time, they let you down. They lose, they get injured, their abilities and dynamics shift.

But God is one whose stats haven't changed since the beginning of time. You can bank on His truth. No surprises. No upsets.

2. *Temptation is common to all.* You may think that temptations only come to those who are weak in faith. You assume that if you can somehow get "spiritual" enough, you won't face the kinds of issues that Joseph faced with Potiphar's wife. But temptation is part of being human. There is no escaping it. First Corinthians 10:13 says, "No temptation has overtaken you except what is common to mankind."

Pursuing godliness doesn't erase your sinful nature. It won't keep you from finding this world appealing. But it will equip you to be obedient to the Word of God.

And God is faithful. He will not allow the temptation to be more than you can stand. When you are tempted, he will show you a way out so that you can endure.
—1 Corinthians 10:13 (NLT)

Jesus Himself was tempted at all points just as you are, yet He remained without sin (Hebrews 4:15). You are not greater than Jesus! So stay close to Him and allow Him to show you the way out.

3. Retreat is often the way to victory. Sometimes you may think you need to conquer temptation or obliterate it completely. Joseph had a different approach: he turned and ran.

Paul told Timothy to flee "youthful lusts" (2 Timothy 2:22 NLT), and in 1 Corinthians he wrote, "Flee from sexual immorality. All other sins a man commits are outside his body, but he who sins sexually sins against his own body" (1 Corinthians 6:18).

Christians, take that verse seriously. Your body is the temple of the Holy Spirit (1 Corinthians 6:19), so if you cross a sexual boundary, you involve the *Holy Spirit.* Sure, in some temptations, you need to stand and fight, but sexual sin is different. In these, you must lace up your fastest track shoes and jet.

One of the worst mistakes you can make is to overestimate your ability to withstand temptation. You think you're bulletproof, and then the next thing you know, you're going to the throne, begging for forgiveness!

The best approach with sexual sin is to have a preventative plan. Your plan may include changing jobs, canceling cable, putting a filter on your internet, not accepting a certain friend request, or avoiding certain spots in town that make you more susceptible to give in. This may sound like a big sacrifice, but take it from God-Inspired Joe: whatever needs to be left behind is worth it for the sake of your integrity.

4. Purity will always be rewarded. This one is tough, because humans tend to want immediate results. Doing the right thing doesn't mean you get rewarded the next day. Don't forget that Joseph sat in prison while Potiphar's wife continued to live in luxury. I'm sure if you were able to ask him if the prison cell was worth it, he'd say, "Yes!" and give you an answer that would sound a lot like Galatians 6:9: "Let us not become weary in doing good, for at the proper time we will reap a harvest if we do not give up."

Joe reaped a harvest at the end of his story, and it saved his family—and a whole nation. That's a reward worth waiting for.

Chapter Four Questions

Question: Look at Joseph's two motivations for remaining pure when faced with fleshly temptation: respect for others and respect for God. How can loving and respecting God and other people help you to make right decisions regarding each of these fleshly desires: premarital/extramarital sex; gambling; internet pornography; alcohol abuse; recreational drugs; overeating?

Question: Have you ever been falsely accused or suffered wrongfully for doing the right thing? How did you respond to this unjust treatment? What were some of the secondary temptations that you faced after responding to the primary temptation correctly?

Question: What character qualities did Joseph have that made Potiphar believe his innocence (and spare his life)? What are some ways you can guard your reputation, and why is this important?

Action: No one—man or woman, old or young, married or single, mature believer or new Christian—is exempt from the temptation to sexual sin. Think through now how you will respond when you are faced with sexual temptation.

- Where are places where you are most likely to encounter temptation?

- What are some situations you can avoid to remove yourself from unnecessary temptation?

- When you are in a vulnerable situation, how can you flee as Joseph did?

Write out your personal purity plan—decisions you are making *now* to guide you in the future as you face temptation.

—

CHAPTER FIVE

The Comeback Kid

I've always felt confident on the basketball court. In fact, in college, I was a bit of a maniac. I hustled like no one else on my team, diving on the floor—resulting in bloody knees and shins after every game. I took charges and flew into the stands on many occasions. As long as I was the one slamming myself on the floor, I didn't care.

There was one game, though, when I experienced a setback. I was sick with a terrible cold and was on so much medicine, I felt like I was going to throw up. I pretended I was fine during the pregame meeting and during warmups, but I worried something awful might happen that would cause me to embarrass my team, my school, and myself. As I ran onto the court, everything felt like a slo-mo dream. *"Stay calm, David, stay calm…. Why do I have to be so sick on game day?"*

Thankfully, nothing horrible happened. In fact, after the adrenaline kicked in, I played one of the best games of my life. Isn't that the way it goes sometimes? You find yourself experiencing a setback, and you assume the worst is happening. But it's not always as it seems.

A String of Setbacks

After the Potiphar debacle, Joseph was given a new residence—a prison cell in Egypt. It wasn't supposed to turn out that way. He had started as the heir to his dad's estate. But then there was that jolting attack by his brothers, the rock-bottom experience in the cistern, and the involuntary relocation to another country. Just when he thought he was settled into a pleasant routine at Potiphar's, he was dealt this latest blow.

If it were you or I sitting there in prison, we might have groaned, "Deal me another hand, Lord. This one is terrible!" You've heard the phrase, "One step forward, two steps back." Joseph's story is more like one step forward, *one hundred* steps back. And yet, he prospered. Why? "The LORD was with Joseph in the prison and showed him his faithful love" (Genesis 39:21 NLT).

G.I. Joe could have been a motivational speaker on how to thrive during setbacks. Can you imagine a workshop entitled *Setback Strategies 101* being offered at your next business conference? I'm fairly sure that would play to an empty room.

Yet you *know* that life is full of setbacks. You just don't want them to happen to *you*. If you haven't experienced one yet, you will. A setback is a lot like a speedbump, but at least a speedbump moves you forward. Setbacks can make you feel like every day is in slo-mo and everyone is getting ahead but you. No matter what it is—a job loss, a broken relationship, a health catastrophe—setbacks are painful! But I believe God allows us to be "dialed back" for His purposes.

Gut Check

More serious than my basketball setback was one I experienced with the birth of my first son, Drew. It's painful to think about it even now, when Drew is a grown man. This setback threw me off my game.

It was November 19, 1990. My wife Suanne and I were living in Tyler, Texas. I was pastoring a church, and Suanne was working as a dental hygienist. We met for lunch that day, but Suanne wasn't feeling well. She was seven months pregnant, so we figured that was the reason. When you're pregnant, you have good days and bad days, right? Perhaps this was just a bad day. After lunch, we both went back to work.

I'll never forget the call that came in around 2:30. It was Suanne's co-worker: "David, you better get down here. She's not good."

Stay Faithful

God was always at work, preparing the way for Joseph to become prime minister of Egypt, but that didn't mean it was going to be a smooth ride. Years went by before the final picture was clear. I wonder what Joseph's talks with God were like when he found himself in prison after the Mrs. Potiphar incident. "God, is this really Your preferred future for me? Were all those dreams just my imagination?"

But even at what seemed to be his lowest point imaginable, Joseph remained faithful to God and put his best foot forward:

> *And the LORD made Joseph a favorite with the prison warden. Before long, the warden put Joseph in charge of all the other prisoners and over everything that happened in the prison. The warden had no more worries, because Joseph took care of everything.*
> **—Genesis 39:21–23** *(NLT)*

Sound familiar? Just like in Potiphar's house, Joseph rose to the top.

Think about the setbacks in your life. How did you get there and journey through them? Who are you today *because* of those setbacks? Who did you meet, and what were you were forced to give up? What was your heart posture during those difficult times? Did you put your best foot forward, even though it felt like you had to limp to do it? Did you stay faithful to God?

Again, with the Dreams

Dreams were a recurring theme with God-Inspired Joe. While in prison, he "just happened" to meet some fellow dreamers. Pharaoh's cupbearer and baker had been thrown in jail for reasons unknown to us. The two prisoners looked a little down one morning—not surprising, since they were in a jail cell—and Joseph noticed.

"Why do you look so worried today?" he asked them. And they replied, "We both had dreams last night, but no one can tell us what they mean."

"Interpreting dreams is God's business," Joseph replied. "Go ahead and tell me your dreams."

—**Genesis 40:7–8** *(NLT)*

Did you catch that? Joe said that interpreting dreams is *God's* business. He revealed *whose business he was on,* right there in jail. That's a great setback strategy!

Have you ever thought, "Hey, I'm in this awful situation, but I'm all about doing God's business?" That would be a great approach. It would help you hold on to hope while He brings you through.

God's Business

The room was silent, except for the sound of the machine that was monitoring our baby's heartbeat. That thing was spitting out yards of tape with information all over it. The doctor's furrowed brow told us that something was horribly wrong.

"We have to get the baby out tonight."

I felt like I'd been tackled in the gut.

That night—I remember it was a Monday because the Raiders were playing the Dolphins on Monday Night Football—our first-born son, Drew, was delivered by emergency C-section.

He was 4.4 pounds. So little. We rejoiced, but he wasn't out of the woods yet.

Setback Strategies 101

If Joseph did teach a workshop about surviving setbacks, he'd include a few of these helpful truths:

1. Setbacks are unexpected. They come at the most unpredictable times and in the most startling ways. They'll come when you're least prepared. People often remark that life is what happens when you're making other plans. My wife and I were making plans to have a baby in a *couple of months,* not that night during Monday Night Football!

You want to live in full expectancy of God's goodness and blessing. But you aren't in heaven yet, so the reality is, you're going to suffer some setbacks. You can often watch as others experience sickness, financial challenges, and loss, but you don't consider that it could ever happen to you. Then—*bam!*

When I officiate at funerals, I notice that people hang on my every word for hope. It's intense. It's as if they suddenly realize this could happen to them or another loved one. And that's true! Why do we cruise along, day after day, assuming we're immune from calamity?

I know God doesn't want us to live in fear every day of our lives, either. A good strategy to stay balanced is to enjoy the problem-free day you are living in, and not fret, yet keep a tight grip on God. He *knows* when your setback is coming. He's a loving Father, and He'll prepare you for it.

2. Setbacks are usually unfair. Sometimes there's an obvious connection between something you did (or didn't do) and your setback, but most of the time, there is no connection at all. Setbacks are random—and just like life, they can seem unfair.

Pete Romero was a star athlete in track and field who shared his story at a men's event at our church. His father kicked him out of the home when Pete didn't want to leave school to work on the farm. Pete knew that he had a future in track and field, and he felt led to hold on to that dream. Thankfully, his high school track coach gave him a place to stay. The only catch was that he had to adapt to some new house rules: get up at 5 a.m. and run five miles. Every day.

Instead of throwing in the towel and saying that life is unfair, Pete rose to the challenge and ended up setting—and breaking—many long-distance records.

Life is filled with challenges and trials, and most of the time, you can't make sense out of why things are happening to you. That's okay. You don't need to have it all figured out. That's God's job.

3. Setbacks are best dealt with by faith. As a child of God, you long to hear His voice and obey Him. But sometimes it's hard. You're tempted to doubt God, especially when you're hit with a setback.

God promises to be with you all the way through your journey. He'll be there when you're in the prison cell, just as He'll be there when you've reached the finish line. Later in life, I believe, Joseph might have said to his family, "I didn't see this blessing coming then, but now I understand, and I always believed God was doing something." That's faith.

When Fear and Confusion Beckon

"He's really fussy. Are new babies supposed to be this fussy?" Suanne rocked our little Drew back and forth and comforted him, as any new mother would. But Drew wouldn't settle. "Something's wrong. We need to get him to a doctor."

He'd already been to plenty of doctors. The night he was born, they had flown him by helicopter to a hospital in Dallas, where a team of doctors looked him over. He'd spent two weeks in the NICU there.

Back to the doctor we went, and we learned the reason for Drew's fussiness: he had meningitis. So it was back to Dallas, where they put him on a machine to keep him alive. Then his lung collapsed. One of the doctors asked me, "You're a preacher, right?" When I said yes, he said, "Then you better start praying."

Drew remained in the hospital in Dallas for two weeks. During one of his exams, the doctor pulled out a measuring tape. He measured Drew's head three times, as if the number he kept coming up with would change. Once again, a doctor's furrowed brow told us that this ordeal was far from over. Away we went to the imaging department, where they discovered a frightening development: Drew had hydrocephalus, and our tiny newborn son needed surgery to survive.

Thankfully, we didn't have the internet or smartphones back then, so we couldn't Google *hydrocephalus*. But even without Web MD, we experienced fear, confusion, and helplessness. The agony I felt thinking that a surgeon would have to use a saw to open Drew's scalp made me sick. I couldn't eat. I couldn't sleep. Activity swirled around me, but I was stuck in slo-mo, like when I was in that basketball game on cold meds. Adrenaline pumped through my system. I was ready to do *anything* to care for my family. Take a charge, hit the ground, end up with bleeding shins and knees, hustle, defend, whatever. But this wasn't *my* game.

"Why does this have to happen to my son, Lord? Please help him!"

A Setback Is a Setup for a Comeback

I believe Joseph would wrap up his fascinating workshop with this statement: *A setback is a setup for a comeback!* His life proved it. Every step of Joe's journey kept him on the path that led to the realization of his God-given dreams. And though the road was rocky and *full* of setbacks, Joe responded by putting his best foot forward. He was truly the Comeback Kid!

Whether he was a slave, a houseboy, a prisoner, or a leader, Joseph gave everything he had for God's glory. As Colossians 3:23 tells us, "Whatever you do, work at it with all your heart, as working for the Lord, not for men."

Friend, God is setting you up for a comeback. Knowing that truth can help you put your best foot forward while you are riding out your setback. And don't *ever* give up! Joseph overcame every temptation, including the temptation to quit. He was patient and persistent, trusting God with the rest. Galatians 6:9 says, "Let us not become weary in doing good." It's a message that you can put into practice even when life sends setbacks.

I also love how in the midst of all his setbacks, Joseph acknowledged the Lord. When the woman tempted him, when he interpreted dreams, and when he was brought before the most powerful man in the world, Joseph was clear that he was a servant of God. It was God who interpreted dreams, imparted wise counsel, and met every single need. Joseph willingly shared what he had received from God and, by doing so, brought blessings to others.

> *Trust in the LORD with all your heart and lean not on your own understanding; in all your ways acknowledge him, and he will make your paths straight.*
> **—Proverbs 3:5–6**

Can you trust God, even when you don't understand? Will you look for that straight path of blessing even though the way seems impossible? Joseph wasn't the only Comeback Kid. You'll be one, too. And when you realize that your setback is just a setup for your comeback, you'll approach each day a little differently, giving God the glory and blessing all those around you.

God Is Bigger

Drew went into surgery. They needed to put a shunt in his brain to relieve the pressure. It was the first of many surgeries, and I never got used to the feeling of helplessness before each one. Yes, I trusted God, but He and I had some lively conversations—one in particular when I unleashed some harsh words that I wouldn't want my congregation to hear.

But God is bigger than words. He's bigger than fear and setbacks. He knows what He's doing with us. And one day during this setback, I *thought* God had given me a clue to His purpose.

I picked up the phone and called my dad, who was a senior pastor at a church in Oklahoma City. "Dad, can I come work for you at the church as your youth pastor? I want our family to live close so our son can spend time with his grandparents."

Silence on the other end. Then, a choked-up voice. "Son, I'd love to have you here. In fact, we need you here. But I can't. We don't have the money in the budget. I'm so sorry."

WORKBOOK

Chapter Five Questions

Question: Describe a season in your life when you faced one setback or difficulty after the next—when it seemed there was nothing else that could go wrong. How did that season change your direction, and how did it change you? How can you see that God was at work through your difficulties?

Question: Do you feel angry, surprised, or threatened by setbacks? What can you do when things are going well to prepare for the suffering that inevitably comes as part of life? How can you become strong in your faith *now* so that future setbacks will help your faith grow, not falter?

Question: Are you a Colossians 3:23 worker? Do you do all your work as if it's for the Lord? What are some areas in which you need to improve when it comes to being a whole-hearted, Christ-centered worker? When your tasks are difficult, demanding, or draining, how can you keep a Colossians 3:23 perspective?

Action: Make a list of the different roles and responsibilities in your life—family, employment, church, volunteering, and even chores, such as "shopper at [store]." Beside each, write out one or more ways you can acknowledge the Lord in that part of your life. Choose one or two ideas from your list to focus on implementing this week, and continue to work your way through the list, acknowledging God "in all your ways" (Proverbs 3:6).

CHAPTER SIX

Power Up

One of the biggest mistakes you can make when beginning a fitness plan is to overdo it on the first day. It usually happens on the second of January, after you've fought the huge crowd into the gym. Then you observe out-of-shape people over in the corner, lifting puny weights.

"I'm in better shape than they are, and I used to lift weights *much* heavier than that ten years ago," you tell yourself. You grab your bicep and squeeze. "I've *still* got it." Then you step up to the weight rack and work up a sweat throwing several fifty-pounders on each side of the barbell. You bend over, grab the bar, grunt like a power-lifter, and pull.

No need to go into what happens next. But it usually involves ice, bottles of Ibuprofen, a few days off work, and the expiration of your thirty-day trial gym membership.

Why do we think strength can be gained in a day?

It can't. Gaining strength takes time and intense training. If given the choice, most of us would skip the process—so God forces it for our own good.

Steps to Strength

Joseph's move from prisoner to Pharaoh's assistant *did* happen in one day, but the training process for that royal position was oh so slow. Remember one step forward, one-hundred steps back? G.I. Joe didn't take *any* steps forward in prison. Sure, he worked hard and exhibited integrity, but that got him noticed by the warden who put him in charge of all the prisoners! Genesis 39:23 says, "The warden had no more worries, because Joseph took care of everything." I'm sure the warden had *no* plans to get rid of Joseph. He was making his job easier! If anything, Joseph was taking steps *in concrete* that would cement him in that prison forever.

The Bible records that after Joseph had been in prison for "some time," two officials of Pharaoh were brought to the prison and were placed under his care. The cupbearer and the baker had offended their master, and the Bible again mentions that they remained in prison for "quite some time." What is quite some time? Weeks? Months? Years? It wasn't until quite some time that the baker and the cupbearer had dreams they didn't understand. When Joseph interpreted their dreams correctly, it looked like he finally *might* take a couple of steps up, at least. Though the baker didn't make it out alive, the cupbearer was restored to his position within three days! All Joe asked of the cupbearer was: "When all goes well with you, remember me and show me kindness; mention me to Pharaoh and get me out of this prison" (Genesis 40:14).

All *did* go well with the cupbearer. "The chief cup-bearer, however, did not remember Joseph; he forgot him" (Genesis 40:23). He forgot him. For two years! Let that sink in. Two years. That's twenty-four months more that Joseph remained in that jail, serving the prisoners. Since *we* know the whole story, it's easy for us to cheer him on. "Hang on, Joe! It's only two more years." But Joseph didn't know God's timetable. He must have prayed every night that God would jog the memory of the cupbearer. Or perhaps he prayed that the cupbearer would offend Pharaoh again and be thrown in jail so they could have a little talk. "Remember me, cup-bearer? I gave you one job…."

But time marched on, and nothing happened.

"Wait" Training

Joseph had no choice but to wait for a breakthrough. That was his training. Day in, day out, serving prisoners, praying, remembering the dreams God had given him. God didn't waste a moment of his life. During the waiting, Joseph became strong.

I've never met a person who likes to wait. And our high-tech world is not making it any easier. I remember the days when I had to wait a whole week for my favorite TV show to come on. Now we can download anything we want to watch, immediately! We have apps for all our favorite food places, so all we need to do is order, skip the line, and there's a bag of our favorite goodies ready with our name on it! We can order something online and get it the next day. Sometimes we can get it *that* day. It's creepy! Who's packing and delivering this stuff so fast? Aliens using underground tunnels? No wonder we overdo our physical training. We're used to getting immediate results from everything else in life.

And then we find ourselves in situations that are on God's timetable. Anyone who's been there will tell you God is *not in a hurry.* That's because He cares more about strengthening you than He does about how long it takes to strengthen you. In fact, *it's in the waiting* that you gain the strength:

> But those who hope in the LORD will renew their strength; they will soar on wings like eagles; they will run and not grow weary, they will walk and not be faint.
> **—Isaiah 40:31**

Waiting on God built Joseph. Waiting on God builds us.

> Wait patiently for the LORD. Be brave and courageous. Yes, wait patiently for the LORD.
> **—Psalm 27:14** (NLT)

In the Midst of Waiting

When I got the news from my dad that he couldn't afford to hire me, I can't say that my initial reaction was "Oh good, God is making me wait, and that's going to make me strong." Yes, I knew God was in control, but at that moment I was discouraged, frustrated, and just plain sad! Have you ever felt that way, even though you knew God was in control? These are human emotions that God understands, and if you are careful to listen during these times, you'll hear his voice. "I'm here. I'm working things out. This is part of your training." And when He finally allows that breakthrough, you'll find you have more compassion, more understanding, and more patience with those who are in the midst of waiting.

One week after that disappointing talk with my dad, a miracle happened. A rich oilman who was a member of my dad's church died in a car crash. That's not the miracle. The miracle is that his wife gave a tithe to the church on the amount she received from the life insurance company. This time the phone call went like this:

"David, would you like to come to Oklahoma City and be my youth pastor? We can afford you now."

"Yes, I would love to come. Thanks, Dad." *And thank You, God!*

My situation changed *in one week.* We didn't have to think or pray much about the decision to move. God had miraculously opened a door, so we packed up, said goodbye to our life in Tyler, and headed to Oklahoma City, where I was installed as the youth pastor at my dad's church.

The only funny thing was, I didn't like teenagers.

Clearly, God had some *more* waiting and strengthening in mind for me.

WORKBOOK

Chapter Six Questions

Question: Are you waiting on something that's on God's timetable right now? What is it? How long have you been waiting for a breakthrough? Jot down ways in which God has and is strengthening you through the process. If you can't think of anything, ask someone who knows you and the situation well. You may be surprised what they see in you!

Question: We tend to become self-focused when we are in a waiting situation. Is there some new way you can serve others while you wait? Joseph served the warden by taking care of all the prisoners, and he used his God-given ability to interpret dreams for the baker and the cupbearer. Has God given you a gift that you have shelved because you are spending too much time focused on your situation? Ask God to reveal how He can use that gift to bless others.

Question: Have you ever tried to imagine what God could be doing in your life through your situation? If you haven't read all the way through the Joseph story, begin today! Write down ways God was preparing Joseph for his palace position with Pharaoh. Do you see any parallels in your own life?

Action: Take some time to look back on your life and recount some of your waiting times and subsequent breakthroughs. What did God do? How long did it take? How are you stronger because of it? Share your story with a friend. It will encourage them, and you, too!

CHAPTER SEVEN

Moving Up

If you've ever been called into the boss's office, you know the feeling of uneasiness that settles in the pit of your stomach. The sweaty palms, the racing heart. You're excited and nervous at the same time as you argue with yourself over whether it's going to be good news or bad news.

One day, while he was busy serving the prisoners, Joseph was called to appear before Pharaoh. The ruler of Egypt was having vivid dreams, and his best advisors had been unable to interpret them.

Remember Joseph's forgetful friend, the cupbearer? Well, he had a conveniently timed memory adjustment:

Then the chief cupbearer said to Pharaoh, "Today I am reminded of my shortcomings. Pharaoh was once angry with his servants, and he imprisoned me and the chief baker in the house of the captain of the guard. Each of us had a dream the same night, and each dream had a meaning of its own. Now a young Hebrew was there with us, a servant of the captain of the guard. We told him our dreams, and he interpreted them for us, giving each man the interpretation of his dream. And things turned out exactly as he interpreted them to us. I was restored to my position, and the other man was hanged."

—Genesis 41:9–13

Isn't it *amazing* how the cupbearer remembered that miraculous story once it might get him in good with his boss?

Well, who cares about the cupbearer? Things were looking up for Joseph!

We soon find out that Joseph hasn't changed at all in two years. He was still working hard and giving God all the credit. When Pharaoh asked him to interpret his dreams, Joseph said the same thing he told the cupbearer and baker two years earlier:

"I cannot do it," Joseph replied to Pharaoh, "but God will give Pharaoh the answer he desires."

—Genesis 41:16

That's a bold statement. Joseph says *he* can't do it. That's not something anyone else in the kingdom would be comfortable telling a frustrated Pharaoh. In fact, that may be why the cupbearer suddenly remembered Joseph. He certainly didn't want to say that *he* couldn't interpret Pharaoh's dreams. That could get him executed.

Pharaoh told Joseph all about his dreams. They were just as fascinating as Joe's dreams from his childhood, and they had that prophetic feel to them, too. Only instead of bundles of wheat bowing down to other bundles of wheat,

Pharaoh's dreams included scrawny cows eating fat cows and thin heads of grain gobbling up plump heads. No wonder he was disturbed!

God-Inspired Joe knew just what the dreams meant. He explained to Pharaoh that there would be seven years of plenty in Egypt, followed by seven years of dire famine (Genesis 41:25–32). He also told him that the events had been "firmly decided by God" (verse 32), who would soon make them happen!

But Joseph didn't stop there. In a courageous move, he went on to suggest what Pharaoh should do about the dream:

> And now let Pharaoh look for a discerning and wise man and put him in charge of the land of Egypt. Let Pharaoh appoint commissioners over the land to take a fifth of the harvest of Egypt during the seven years of abundance. They should collect all the food of these good years that are coming and store up the grain under the authority of Pharaoh, to be kept in the cities for food. This food should be held in reserve for the country, to be used during the seven years of famine that will come upon Egypt, so that the country may not be ruined by the famine.
>
> **—Genesis 41:33–36**

Joseph handed Pharaoh his future job description! Who else was as discerning and wise as Joe at that moment? How could Pharaoh afford *not* to hire him? I like what Pharaoh asked his officials: "Can we find anyone else like this man so obviously filled with the spirit of God?" (Genesis 41:38 NLT).

The answer was no. By the end of their meeting, Joseph

had been appointed as Pharaoh's second-in-command (Genesis 41:39–40).

Power Perks

In a moment, Joseph went from the lowest of the low to the second most powerful man in that land. And that came with a whole list of perks:

- Limitless territorial control. No one could lift a finger without consulting Joseph first.

- A shiny new chariot.

- Pharaoh's signet ring, which granted him unlimited buying power.

- An expensive wardrobe.

- Fame.

- Clout.

- A wife!

- A new place to live. No more prison (poor warden).

- A new name. Pharaoh gave Joseph the name Zaphenath-paneah, which may refer to the revealing of secrets or could mean something like "God speaks and lives" (Genesis 41:45 NLT).

Things were looking up for God-Inspired Joe. You

could say the guy came into Pharaoh's office empty and left carrying a full cup. What would happen next?

The Pitfalls of Success

Success is the American dream. It's what we all strive for, but it can bring challenges that can tear us down. We all know people who, amid blessing and success, were tripped up by their achievements. I think of President Nixon, whose choices forced him to resign from the presidency or face impeachment. Mike Tyson, the heavyweight champion of the world, became a convicted sex offender. The baseball player Pete Rose had a gambling addiction. Elvis Presley died from a combination of drugs and alcohol. Michael Jackson, Tiger Woods, and many others throughout history have found that the American dream can quickly become a nightmare.

You see this in the Bible, too. Scripture gives examples of those who crumbled spiritually under the pressure of success. King Saul started off so humble that he couldn't be found at his own inauguration (1 Samuel 10:21–22). Yet years later he became so arrogant that he usurped the authority of the high priest and offered sacrifices to God unlawfully (1 Samuel 13:8–9). King David is described as a man after God's own heart (1 Samuel 13:14), but later in his life, he committed adultery, plotted to have a man murdered, and then did everything he could to cover it all up (2 Samuel 11–12). King Solomon humbly asked God for wisdom (1 Kings 3:6–9), but after several years in power became foolish, immoral, and hedonistic.

We are all susceptible to allowing success to get the best of us. Scripture warns us of some major pitfalls of success:

1. Pride. Solomon wrote, "Pride goes before destruction" (Proverbs 16:18). Success can make you overconfident and sure of yourself. That confidence can lead you to think that you're better than other people You've heard sports figures trash talk another team, only to be beaten the next game they play against them. Hollywood stars use their platforms to bash those serving in government and lose fans because of it. Businesswoman Leona Hemsley owned millions in real estate but refused to pay income tax and famously said, "We don't pay taxes. Only the little people pay taxes."[7]

It's always refreshing to hear stories of those who can stay humble in the midst of success. Those who knew him well say that Sam Walton drove the same pickup, drank coffee in the same coffee shops, and treated people the same way he had before he saw success.[8]

2. Indulgence. In Luke 16, Jesus tells a parable about a rich man who lived luxuriously and a poor man who subsisted on the scraps from the rich man's table. When both men died, the rich man faced torment in hell while the poor man was carried to Abraham's side. It's a powerful reminder that those of us who have extra are responsible to use those resources to bless others.

The missionary Albert Schweitzer was an unpretentious man. He had one hat and one black tie, which he wore every day. He didn't need more, so he didn't take more.[9] When he learned of a co-worker who owned a dozen ties, his response was, "For one neck?" Contrast that with the televangelist who lives in opulence. One is out serving; the other is seemingly out to be served. Indulgence can entrap any heart that clings to the riches of this world.

3. False security. Success can trick you into thinking that you don't need help. You can become convinced that you can do it all on your own, and this conviction strips away your trust in God. Job reminds us: "Naked I came from my mother's womb, and naked I will depart. The LORD gave and the LORD has taken away; may the name of the LORD be praised" (Job 1:21).

4. Laziness. A successful person can become so sure in his ways that he doesn't even try anymore. I've seen this in athletes and in successful businesspeople. They think they have it all figured out and slip into what's comfortable. They avoid risk. They do just the opposite of what they did to get them to the top of the success ladder! Laziness is dangerous for a child of God, since He wants you to stretch, grow, and take new steps in the direction of your calling.

5. Distraction. Many times, someone will come to me with a great need—a job, an illness, or some debt trouble. They want me to pray; they want me to be in the trenches with them and help guide them through with spiritual counsel.

Six months later, their problem is solved and they're living large. They've got a new car or a bigger house. And their focus shifts from spiritual things to worldly things.

This pitfall is a top threat to any believer. "Some people, eager for money, have wandered from the faith and pierced themselves with many griefs" (1 Timothy 6:10). Our success can distract us and pull us away from what *really* matters.

The Cure for Success

J. Oswald Sanders said, "Not everyone can carry a full cup"—but Joseph did.[10] Genesis 41:46 says, "Joseph was thirty years old when he entered the service of Pharaoh king of Egypt. And Joseph went out from Pharaoh's presence and traveled throughout Egypt." What a way to begin! And from then on, you never see Joseph distracted, lazy, or thinking he was better than anyone else. His great attitude and faithfulness to God's leading led to solid actions that give us some great examples to learn from today.

1. Joseph accepted his position willingly. He didn't run from it or make excuses. He wasn't insecure or fearful. He didn't apologize for God's blessing in his life, either. He lived by the belief that if God promotes you, there is no need to feel guilty about it. He understood that a blessing upon his life meant he could extend blessings to others.

2. Joseph was diligent for a prolonged period. He knew how to delegate and organize people, but he also knew how to put in the hard work. If you just look at the action verbs of his story, you find that he went out, he traveled, he collected, he stored, and he kept records (Genesis 41:46–49). Joseph wasn't just a figurehead; he was a worker who did his absolute best to please his Lord.

3. Joseph married one woman and remained faithful his entire life. How different would his life have been had Joseph given in to Potiphar's wife? Instead, even in a culture where men had many wives, Joseph was able to honor God in his marriage relationship. Proverbs 5:15 says, "Drink water from your own well—share your love only with your wife" (NLT). God's best is always reserved for those who do things His way.

4. Joseph used his position to benefit other people. In one of the biggest twist endings in the Bible, Joseph reconciled with his family and provided for them until the day he died (Genesis 46–50). His ability to forgive is a sign of true humility, and in God's kingdom, that's what leads to greatness.

5. Joseph remembered God and gave Him the credit. In everything he did, Joseph pointed toward God. Even the names of his children were reminders of what God was doing and had done in Joseph's life! *Manasseh* comes from the word that means "forget suffering," while *Ephraim* means "fruitfulness"—true tributes to the way God had blessed Joseph in a foreign country (Genesis 41:51–52).

A Humble Heart

The world tells you that when you've achieved success it's okay to be prideful and self-assured. It encourages self-belief and rejects dependence on others. But God seeks a humble heart. He has great plans for you, but it is only in your dependence on Him that those plans can be realized.

Like Joseph, you must rely on God even when you find yourself in a downpour of blessing. Give God the credit, as all good and perfect things come from Him. Read your Bible, seek His face, and serve in humility whether you are the CEO of a powerful company or a worker on a factory floor. You may be ridiculed. You may not fit in, but just like Joseph, you don't have to compromise your beliefs. You can live as a true example of what it means to follow God in *everything,* trusting that He holds the world in His hands.

A New Assignment

Accepting my new assignment as youth pastor in Oklahoma City tested my courage. Since I had already been serving as a senior pastor, I could have been tempted to see this bend in the path as a speedbump or setback. But it was neither. It was a blessing. I found out that teenagers are not so bad after all. (Though, yes, they are loud and unpredictable—and messy. And goofy). I learned some helpful skills that would shape my ministry in the future. I was thankful for God's orchestration that had brought us to Oklahoma City. And we were encouraged by the close presence of family, which had always held a particular value for me, placed deep in my heart by my loving Heavenly Father.

To my surprise, it was a restful time for me. I had been preaching for nine years up to this point, and I didn't realize how much I needed a break to refresh and restore my passion. As I sat and listened to my dad preach every week, God was building me up and renewing my call. And it was true joy to witness my son Drew begin to form an unbreakable bond with my dad that remains to this day. If success is achieving what we hope for, then I was experiencing it. By following a bend in the road, we were moving up in life.

WORKBOOK

Chapter Seven Questions

Question: Success—even when given by God—can become the source of our undoing. Why do you think success is such a danger? Who have you known who has handled success wisely, and what do you think made them able to do so?

Question: What are some areas where you are tempted toward indulgence or extravagance? Do you ever get so focused on minor issues that you lose sight of people facing real problems such as disease, poverty, hunger, and war? How can you remain balanced and compassionate in your use of the resources God has given you?

Question: Do you depend fully on God even when things are going great? How do you intentionally give Him the credit for your talents and successes? How will you embrace the promotions that God gives you without allowing pride to wreck you?

Action: Read Mark 10:45. Is your mindset one of seeking to serve or seeking to be served? What are some avenues of service that you can be involved in, to help you remain humble and focused on others versus yourself? (Consider "unglamorous" and unsung service opportunities such as serving at a rescue mission or homeless shelter, working in the church nursery, or cleaning up after a large outreach event.) Make one of these types of service a regular part of your life and ask God to use it to help you manage your success and blessings in a way that glorifies Him.

CHAPTER EIGHT

Reject Revenge

A woman called her husband while he was driving home from work. She wanted to warn him about a dangerous situation she had seen on the news—a driver was heading the wrong way down the highway. Her husband yelled in response, "Dear, it's not just one—there are hundreds of them heading in the wrong direction!"

With all of the traffic, congestion, and bottlenecks on our roads these days, sometimes it can feel like we're surrounded by a bunch of crazed idiots! It's enough to turn a calm, civilized, person into a road-raged maniac. I think of Sophocles' ancient Greek tragedy *Oedipus Rex*, in which the character Oedipus recounts, "As the charioteer lurched over towards me, I struck him in my rage...." Oedipus killed a man for his bad driving skills![11]

Hopefully, you've never assaulted someone for swerving into your lane or cutting you off on the road. Yet I dare you to take a moment and think about how you react when you are wronged. Do you graciously let the perceived injustice slide? Or do you lash out?

If we're honest, most of us feel like that husband. We look at people around us and assume that it's the other guy who is at fault. It's the *other guy* who caused the mess we're in. We even plot ways to get back at the people we believe have wronged us. We may not go as far as Oedipus did with the chariot driver, but there are times when we're tempted to stoop to new lows just for revenge.

The road of life is filled with all kinds of traffic, infractions, and even a few accidents now and then. If you're not careful about your response, you can experience a spiritual road rage that is just as dangerous.

Here's Your Chance, Joe!

If anyone in the Bible could have been the poster child for road rage, it would be Joseph. He was picked on, beaten up, sold into slavery, falsely accused, thrown into prison, forgotten by his friends—yet he refused to focus on revenge when his brothers came to Egypt looking for food

For seven years, just as Joseph had predicted, the land produced a huge harvest. And, at Joseph's direction, Egypt gathered all the crops and stored the grain to prepare for the coming famine. Genesis 41:49 says, "He piled up huge amounts of grain like sand on the seashore." That's a lot of grain! Verse 49 also says, "Finally, he stopped keeping records because there was too much to measure." There would be no hunger pangs in Egypt with God-Inspired Joe at the helm.

But there *would* be hunger pangs in neighboring countries, and all would come to buy grain from Joseph. Another benefit for Egypt! They not only ate well during the famine; they made a fortune.

In the land of Canaan, people were starving, too. Specifically, the members of Joseph's family. It got so bad that Jacob sent the ten oldest brothers to Egypt to buy grain, and we all know *who* they had to talk to about that.

This is the point in the story where you may want to pound the table and yell, "*Yes!* Finally! Get 'em, Joseph! Make 'em starve! Get back at them for all they did to you!" If this were a movie scene, the director would cue the intense music, harsh words, and loud weeping and wailing. Then Joseph would walk away victorious, washing his hands of his hateful brothers. Forever.

But that's not how it went down. Joseph must have been tempted to take revenge after all his brothers had done to him. Instead, he rejected that approach. Why? Genesis 42:6 says, "When Joseph's brothers arrived, they bowed down to him with their faces to the ground. As soon as Joseph saw his brothers, he recognized them." Did his heart race? You bet it did. The verse continues by saying that "he pretended to be a stranger and spoke harshly to them." Joseph was probably close to losing it!

But then Genesis 42:9 says this: "Then he remembered his dreams about them." You know the dreams—for instance, the one where the brothers' bundles of grain bowed down to his bundle of grain. Joseph was beginning to see the big picture.

Revenge Feels Right

The desire for revenge is natural to the human condition. Just look at how many popular movies revolve around the topic. Almost every Clint Eastwood film is about the main character exacting revenge on some low-life scum. "Go ahead, make my day!" is a famous quoted line. And we all know what it means. "You deserve to die, punk, so just give me a reason to pull this trigger."

Everybody is getting revenge in movies: Dirty Harry, the Sith, and even the Nerds. We love to watch—and often cheer them on. People even look to the Old Testament for justification for revenge.

> *But if there is serious injury, you are to take life for life, eye for eye, tooth for tooth, hand for hand, foot for foot, burn for burn, wound for wound, bruise for bruise.*
> *—Exodus 21:23–25*

The meaning of this passage is mistaken by many. It was never meant to encourage personal retribution. This passage describes part of a legal system—the judicial code for Israel. It didn't mean that if something happened and you lost an eye, you had the right to go and take someone else's eye. Specifically, it addressed the consequences for accidental injury to a pregnant woman that resulted in a premature birth. In general, it expressed the principle that you had the right to take someone to court and if the court found that person guilty, he or she would receive a judgment.

Leviticus 19:18 says, "Do not seek revenge or bear a

grudge ... but [instead] love your neighbor as yourself." Joseph had every right to take his brothers to the court, but instead decided to focus on reconciliation and love.

A Better Way

Joe was not only faithful, hard-working, and God-honoring, he was also clever! He knew he needed time to discover if his brothers were the same jealous, angry people that he had known all those years ago. So, he devised a plan. How he did it while the emotions were swirling is beyond me. But remember, the Lord was with Joseph, and the Lord is *always* about reconciliation.

"You are spies! You have come to see how vulnerable our land has become" (Genesis 42:9 NLT). After questioning the brothers about their family and where they lived, Joseph insisted Simeon stay with him, while sending the others away with all the grain they had requested. To release Simeon, Joseph demanded they bring back the brother who had *not* come to Egypt: Benjamin (Genesis 42:33–34). Joseph also ordered his servants to fill the brothers' grain sacks, but to secretly return each payment by placing it at the top of the sack. When the brothers discovered this while on their journey home, their hearts sank. How could they break all this bad news to their father?

Jacob, of course, was livid: "You are robbing me of my children! Joseph is gone! Simeon is gone! And now you want to take Benjamin, too. Everything is going against me!" (Genesis 42:36 NLT).

An interesting dynamic begins to form here in what appears to be a downhill slide for the family. This dysfunctional, self-serving, prideful bunch begins to support one another and work together. Reuben steps up and takes personal responsibility for Benjamin's safety. That's new! But Jacob waits and worries. Then the grain runs out and Jacob panics some more. This time Judah steps up and guarantees Benjamin's safety.

I wonder what Joseph was thinking while he was waiting for the brothers' return. *"Will they even come back? Do they care about their brother, Simeon, who is stuck here in prison? Will they leave him here and forget about him, just like they did to me?"* The desire to take revenge must have risen many times in Joseph's heart. He could have done anything to them—he had so much power!

But he waited and didn't do what merely felt right in the moment. He chose a better way, and that gave God time to work.

A Perfect Judge

God is the only perfect judge, and when you demand retribution, you take judgment out of God's hands. It's not your job to administer justice or determine who gets punished and who gets a pass, because God already has that covered. He created the judicial system here on earth to handle physical, earthly offenses, but He is judge and jury of the heavenly realm, where He handles spiritual wrongdoings.

"Revenge is sweet" is a popular saying, but if you talk to anyone who has exacted revenge, they will tell you the opposite. It may feel good in the moment, but after a while, it turns sour!

I think of Peter in the garden of Gethsemane. He was ready to get revenge for what the soldiers were about to do to his Lord. But Jesus stopped him (John 18:10–11). In effect, Jesus said, "Hold on, Peter. You're going to mess up my plan. I'm about to redeem the whole world. Put your sword away."

God knows and sees everything. He knows the intricate details of all your problems. He knows who has hurt you, and asks, "Do you trust Me to take care of this? Will you wait for Me to move?" When you take revenge, you are answering Him with a resounding, "No!"

The Bible is clear: God will enact absolute justice for the whole universe (see Ecclesiastes 3:17). I think Joseph understood this. He knew that if he stepped in—if he meddled—he'd be imposing himself on God's plan. He saw that God was working on his brothers just as He was working on Joseph. He trusted the process. He trusted Almighty God, and he was a living example of Romans 12:19, "Do not take revenge, my friends, but leave room for God's wrath."

Circular Grace

Have you ever hurt anybody? Think about that for a minute. Life can be a struggle, and sometimes we don't always love people well. Could your name be on someone's "list" for revenge? How would you like them to handle that?

We are all guilty. God, our perfect judge, knows all

about it. But instead of giving you what you deserve—death and eternal separation from Him—he extends grace to you through Jesus Christ.

If God has been gracious to you, can you then be gracious to others?

Has somebody wronged you? Has a family member hurt you? Has a friend gossiped about you? Has someone stolen something valuable, or stepped on your toes?

Jesus said in Matthew 5:44, "Love your enemies and pray for those who persecute you." When you reject revenge, you're stepping into the cycle of grace. It's a beautiful, circular pattern. You're surrendering to His power, and that puts your heart in a position to forgive.

Slamming Doors

If someone slams a door in your face, you might be tempted to punch right through it. But consider this: God might want that door closed.

After I had served for almost two years as my dad's youth pastor in Oklahoma City, a preaching position opened up for me in Union, Missouri. We accepted that call, knowing it was just a few hours from family, and because it fell more closely in line with God's calling on my life. The church was small, but God brought blessing and growth to the congregation while I was there. He also brought growth and blessing to us personally. Little Zach joined our family on December 1, 1993.

Soon after we brought Zach home, we began to realize that the little upstairs apartment the church had provided for us was not going to work well for our family. And since I felt so good about our partnership there and the future of the ministry, I boldly asked the elders for some help with a down payment on a house, with the understanding that we would pay it back as soon as possible, or worst-case scenario, we'd pay it back when we sold the house.

Their answer? No! And not *just* no. It was *never.* "We will *never* do that kind of thing. So just put it out of your mind. It's not happening."

Wham—door slam! I was stunned by their answer. It hurt. And I had an immediate decision to make about my response. I wanted to punch back. It felt right at that moment. They wanted me to take care of everyone but didn't want to take care of us. Revenge, let's see... What can a pastor do to get revenge?

Nothing. I couldn't call myself their pastor and go in that direction. This was not my fight. And after all the speedbumps and setbacks I had already experienced, I knew this had to be part of God's big picture. Busting through the current closed door could thwart His plan. So I prayed, I waited, and I gave the best I could under the circumstances. I figured I'd eventually save the money needed, and then I'd find a more suitable place for my family to live.

About a month later, a church in Downey, California, called me. My brother Dudley had given them my name. They wanted me to be their preacher, and they were willing to double my current salary. On top of that, they offered $1,300 to rent a house with a heated swimming pool.

This was about to get interesting.

WORKBOOK

Chapter Eight Questions

Question: Have you ever been tempted to seek revenge? Did you go through with your desire? If so, how did you feel after you had enacted your revenge? If not, what stopped you? How can you, like Joseph, work through the *feelings* of revenge while leaving your offender unharmed?

Question: What are some ways that God has filled your life with mercy and grace? Why and how can you also show undeserved kindness to those who have wronged you?

Question: Joseph's father Jacob had been on the receiving end of forgiveness from a wronged brother who initially desired revenge. How might the example of Jacob's and Esau's reconciliation in Genesis 33 (which Joseph would have been old enough to have understood and remembered) have inspired Joseph's own treatment of his brothers? Who in your own life has been an example of forgiveness?

Action: What do you think led to the changes in Joseph's brothers' hearts? Read Genesis 38. How might the events of this story be part of the change in Judah's life? Contrast Judah's actions and attitudes in Genesis 37 with those in Genesis 42 and following.

Write out a specific prayer list for the person(s) upon whom you most want to enact revenge. Commit to praying through your list regularly and asking God to work in them to draw them into a right relationship with Him.

CHAPTER NINE

Foster Forgiveness

We've all been there: Your child doesn't get picked for the team. A friend betrays you. You go through a painful divorce. You discover that lies are being spread about you. A parent or mentor abuses or neglects you. Your adult children cut you off. Your church fails you. You also struggle with painful life experiences that bring bitterness and rejection, and you can find yourself offended and hurt. You have a choice to make. You can work through these feelings with God's grace, or you can let your pain fester and build, resulting in years of resentment and discontent.

Thankfully, Jesus not only comforts you in your affliction, but He also shows you the way to deal with the hurt. His ultimate solution? Forgiveness.

When Jesus taught us how to pray in Matthew 6, He made forgiveness a main focus: "Forgive us our debts, as we also have forgiven our debtors" (Matthew 6:12). If forgiveness was so important to Jesus, shouldn't it be important to you?

It's amazing how petty people can be. Billionaire John Paul Getty rewrote his will over and over, out of mean-spirited amusement.[12] Every time someone so much as irritated him, he simply recalculated their meager portion of his estate. This is no way to live! Yet so many of us likewise keep score in petty ways. You might not be updating your will continuously, but you alter which people you text, limit which people you hang out with, add names to your gossip list, and in general, alter how you do life with people.

You may *say* that you're going to extend grace to someone, but then you hold onto resentment, refusing to completely wipe the slate clean.

All this does is tear down the family of God. And that includes you.

Forgiveness 101

And when you stand praying, if you hold anything against anyone, forgive him, so that your Father in heaven may forgive you your sins.
—Mark 11:25

Forgiveness sounds so simple, yet it's one of the hardest things God calls you to do. Thankfully, your Father knows when it is your sincere desire to forgive someone, and He gives you the power you need to do it. But you do have some steps to take.

Step #1: Release your right to retaliation. Do you realize how many types of retaliation humans are capable of?

There's legal retaliation (a biggie these days). Financial retaliation. Verbal retaliation. There's alliance retaliation. You might have experienced the latter. It's when a person tries to turn as many people as they can against you. Another popular way to retaliate is to ignore someone. Give them the cold shoulder. It's been going on for a long time, but now in the age of social media, "Ghosting" is a popular way to retaliate. Ghosting is the practice of ending a personal relationship with someone by withdrawing all form of communication. Unfriend, unfollow, block, erase all texts, delete all emails—any trace that a person existed in your life. This is how many of our young people are ending their dating relationships! Can you imagine the damage that does to a society—having a good portion of the population walking around hurt, confused, and ill-equipped to work through conflict?

No matter what side of the retaliation you are on, it's never healthy. God knows this; that's why He commands you to *release it*. Holding a grudge, making a person pay, or hoping a person fails just because they have wronged you damages *your heart*: "See to it that no one misses the grace of God and that no bitter root grows up to cause trouble and defile many" (Hebrews 12:15).

Step #2: Do your part to restore the relationship. Sometimes you will claim to forgive a person, but you don't do anything to rebuild the relationship. This one is tough, because what if you reach out and are met with disdain by the other person? What if you take a step to build a bridge and the other person lobs a bomb in your direction? What if you forgive and rebuild, and then the person hurts you again—and again?

It's important to understand the difference between forgiveness and trust. You are called to forgive everyone; you are *not* called to trust everyone. If a young couple is engaged and she cheats on him, then forgiveness is the way of Christ—but I wouldn't recommend that he marry her. She can be forgiven even though she must earn back his trust.

Step #3: Acknowledge the sovereignty of God. A stumbling block for some is the feeling that if they forgive an offense, it would be admitting that what happened didn't matter. Are you supposed to ignore the horrible, unjust things that have been done against you or your loved ones? No. But like Joseph, you can try to understand a much bigger picture.

God cares deeply about everything that hurts and harms you. He longs for a just world in which evil is vanquished. He came to earth, died on that cross, was buried, and then rose again to ensure that one day, those who have put their trust in Him will no longer suffer. But until then, you must trust Him to work all things out for good.

"God Sent Me Here"

Genesis 45 is one of the most emotional chapters in the whole Joseph story. This is when Joseph reveals himself to his brothers. He was a lot older by now—scholars say he was about forty—and he'd been through a lot. It would have been nice to have some family support through it all, but that wasn't what God had planned. And now all his brothers stood in front of him—including Benjamin!

It was all too much for Joseph. The Bible says he sent his attendants out of the room, and he broke down and wept. He wept so hard the Egyptians could hear him, and word of it quickly carried to Pharaoh's palace.

"I am Joseph!" he said to his brothers. There was no harshness in his voice this time, just relief, joy, and forgiveness. So much time had passed. Life had dealt them their share of blows. Joseph had grown through adversity and now had a mature understanding of the meaning of his dreams. And how did Joseph know his brothers were ready for his big reveal? Because they passed his tests.

1. Joseph tested how his brothers would respond under difficult circumstances. After accusing them of being spies, Joseph put his brothers in prison for three days (Genesis 42:9–17). He may have wanted them to consider life with an uncertain future—much like he'd experienced twenty years earlier.

Imagine what the brothers were thinking. They certainly didn't expect this kind of welcome. The brothers spoke among themselves in Joseph's presence: "Surely we are being punished because of our brother. ... Now we must give an accounting for his blood" (Genesis 42:21–22).

The brothers still felt guilt twenty years after their wrongdoing. Their words proved to Joseph that they knew they had done a terrible thing—and for Joseph, it meant moving one step closer to forgiveness.

2. Joseph tested how the brothers would respond when everything went well. When Joe's brothers returned with

Benjamin, he treated them like royalty. He threw a banquet, sat them according to their age, and gave Benjamin five times more food than he gave the others! Sounds a little like the way it had been back in the day when Jacob showed favoritism to Joseph. But none of the brothers complained or showed resentment this time. Instead, they feasted and drank freely. They were not the jealous men they had once been (Genesis 43:31–34).

3. *Joseph tested how the brothers would respond when they were wrongfully accused.* After the feast, Joseph sent his family off, on their journey back home. He instructed his palace manager to hide Joseph's silver cup in Benjamin's sack, and then sent him to chase them down with accusations of robbery (Genesis 44:1–5).

The brothers insisted they had stolen nothing. Then, when Benjamin was found with the cup, they refused to leave his side. They stood by him even when it appeared that he had done a great wrong. They begged and pleaded with Joseph, explaining that they couldn't go home without Benjamin, who was their father's favorite. If they went home without Benjamin, they feared, their father would die. Judah volunteered to receive Benjamin's punishment by taking his place as Joseph's servant. (See Genesis 44:6–34.)

This was the ultimate test, showing Joseph that his brothers' hearts had shifted from a position of selfishness and jealousy to one of love and sacrifice. And it's not surprising that centuries later there would be one from the tribe of Judah who would come and offer His life as a sacrifice for us all.

"I am Joseph!" he said to his brothers. "Is my father still alive?" But his brothers were speechless! They were stunned to realize that Joseph was standing there in front of them. "Please, come closer," he said to them. So they came closer. And he said again, "I am Joseph, your brother, whom you sold into slavery in Egypt. But don't be upset, and don't be angry with yourselves for selling me to this place. It was God who sent me here ahead of you to preserve your lives."

—Genesis 45:3–5 *(NLT)*

What a reunion! It was the culmination of huge speed bumps and unfair setbacks which were all part of a divine setup for a victorious comeback, but *forgiveness* is what made it all possible.

Forgiveness for All

The Nazis brutally mistreated Corrie Ten Boom in a World War II concentration camp.[13] She experienced and witnessed the very worst of mankind, and the crimes committed against her and her family are unthinkable.

A few years after her release, she had a speaking engagement in Munich. She planned to speak on the topic of forgiveness. Afterward, a man approached her—and she recognized him instantly. He was a former prison guard in the camp where she had been enslaved. Of all the guards, he had been the most vile and cruel.

"Can you possibly forgive me?" he asked.

Corrie felt chilled, but she went to shake his hand anyway. Instantly, the warmth of reconciliation washed over her. With utmost sincerity, she said to him, "I forgive you, brother, with my whole heart."

When reflecting on this encounter, Corrie said, "I had never known God's love so intensely as I did then."

You may think the closest you ever get to God is when He forgives you, but I think it's when you forgive others—especially people the world would deem unforgivable. You are never more like Jesus than in those moments.

There is nothing like the joy of true forgiveness. Who needs forgiveness in your life? What past hurts are you holding onto? Take the steps toward forgiveness today.

Chapter Nine Questions

Question: How did Joseph's tests of his brothers mirror the tests that Joseph himself had endured during his time in Egypt? What are some situations where an offender might need to regain trust to bring about reconciliation? How can you extend forgiveness while also being realistic about whether the offender has changed and what the relationship will look like going forward?

Question: What are some situations when you might offer forgiveness but not restoration of the relationship? What are some situations in which there might be limited restoration? How does having realistic expectations about a restored relationship help in fully forgiving the offending person?

Question: Think about a situation in which someone wronged you and you had to make the choice to forgive them. How can you see God's sovereignty over that situation? Are you able to trace ways that what they meant for evil God has used, or can use in the future, for good? Are you willing for your pain to lead to a blessing for others, even if some of those others are the ones who caused the pain?

Action: Read Luke 6:27. What are some examples from the Bible of people who not only forgave their enemies but also did good to them? Take your forgiveness plan a step further. After praying for your offender on a regular basis, ask God for a practical, tangible way in which you can do good for him or her. Enact your plan and journal about it. How is doing good for your enemy a crucial step in the process of full forgiveness?

CHAPTER 10

Finish Strong

As I shared in the intro to this book, I loved to play with G.I. Joes when I was a kid, but I had to borrow them from my brothers. I would have loved to have my very own, brand-new, right-out-of-the-package action figure, but hey, the baby of the family gets hand-me-downs. By the time I got the G.I. Joes, they were beat-up from years of climbing trees, being left outside in the dirt, and hanging off cliffs. The Kung-Fu grip was shredded! But once I started playing, I didn't notice any of those flaws. It didn't matter what Joe had been through—he could still be the hero of any adventure. The guy had guts, muscle, and the push-through attitude to finish every day strong.

That's how I want to live my life. No matter what I've been through, no matter where the speedbumps and setbacks take me, I want to finish strong—for me, my family, and the Lord.

The Next Step

The offer from the Downey church was one we could not pass up. Young ministry families need resources to survive, and God had provided through this generous congregation. California was where my two older brothers were serving as pastors, so that was a plus, too. But it was a long way from my mom and dad, and even after two years of living in Missouri, Drew still cried every time we drove away from a visit with my parents. Would we ever see them living in California? We couldn't afford to buy airline tickets for four of us to fly back and forth all the time. But we prayed, had faith, and took the next step, knowing that God held the desires of our hearts in His loving hands.

A Marathon, Not a Sprint

A cheetah is a fascinating animal. Its body is created for explosive sprints—chase the game and pounce. No animal can beat a cheetah in a sprint.

But if it can dodge, jump, hide, and outsmart him just long enough, he'll survive. Why? Though the cheetah can reach speeds of around 70 mph, it can only sprint about 300 meters before running out of steam. Then it takes him up to thirty minutes to recover. The cheetah can't even eat right after making a kill because it is so exhausted.[14]

We tend to live our lives as if we are in a cheetah-crazed sprint. We drive hard in so many directions, starting one project after another, but then we run out of gas and quit. We're great starters. Not such great finishers.

Friends, this will not work in your spiritual life. God wants you to start the journey with Him by accepting His gift of eternal life through Jesus, but it doesn't stop there. He wants you to continue the journey with Him, up every hill, through every valley, hitting the speedbumps, rolling with the setbacks, and finishing strong! Spiritual life is not a sprint. It's a marathon.

Middle-Aged Joe

We don't have a lot of information about how Joseph lived from age 40 to his death at 110, but we have enough to see that he didn't waver in his commitment to his Lord. He finished strong in three big ways.

1. Joseph took care of his family. After Joseph revealed his identity to his brothers and they had their tearful reunion, Joseph took on some big responsibilities with his family by bringing them to live in his world.

We like to think the family lived happily ever after, like a fairy tale, but I don't think it worked that way. Dysfunctional families don't just change overnight, and it's likely there were real issues that required more and more of Joseph's attention.

Joseph's life was so much different than his family's life. In the process of overseeing an entire country, Joseph had become independently wealthy. He had a wife and kids and had lived many years in the Egyptian culture.

Contrast that with Jacob, who was poor. His family barely survived the first two years of famine, and on top of that, they were members of a despised race. (See Genesis 43:32. Eating with Hebrews was "detestable" to Egyptians.) The family occupation of shepherding was also looked down upon by the refined Egyptians (Genesis 46:34).

Think about it: Joseph had to introduce his unsophisticated, elderly shepherd father to Pharaoh and all his wealthy friends. I can't imagine it was easy for Joseph, but he honored Jacob the best he could. He went out to meet his father when he visited, and he expressed his compassion and showed his emotion in public. Despite all that had happened, he chose to develop a new relationship with his dad.

Joe took great care of his family, giving them the best of his provisions and providing them with a life of luxury. When Jacob died, Joseph set up a seventy-day mourning period throughout Egypt (Genesis 50:2–3). What a model of love and faithfulness! Joseph chose to finish life with a strong relationship with his family, even after everything that had happened.

2. Joseph continued to be productive even after he was successful. They say it's harder to stay on top than to reach the top. When we've finally "made it," we can become comfortable, telling ourselves we deserve a break and should enjoy the fruits of our labor.

Joseph was in a perfect spot to let things go a little. He was wealthy and powerful. No one would have thought anything of it if he would have relaxed a bit. Instead, he chose to remain productive even when he'd reached the very top of his potential.

I'm convinced that the best way to become productive and stay that way in your middle age or older is to get involved in the church. Take part in a ministry and bring intention to that space. While your job may no longer challenge you like it once did, serving people and sharing Jesus with them will fix that right up! A commitment to be a blessing to someone else will give you the fullest, most enriching years of your life.

Contrast that attitude with Jacob's. He was convinced he was going to die. For thirty-seven years, he claimed to have one foot in the grave (Genesis 37:35, 42:38, 44:30–31, 46:30). Then, finally, in Genesis 48:21, he again bemoaned his old age—"I am about to die!"—and it happened.

Can you imagine spending thirty-seven years waiting for death? We might laugh, but people do it all the time. They stop trying, hang up their cleats, and say things like, "Well, it's been a good run," but they're only in their sixties!

I am thankful to have served with so many seniors who were great examples of fruitfulness right up until the day God called them home. And what a homecoming that must have been. They jogged right into heaven, shoes on, ready to continue their strong relationship with their Heavenly Father for eternity.

3. Joseph maintained his faith in God, even in a pagan environment. Egypt was full of false idols and immorality. It couldn't have been easy to maintain faith in God in that kind of environment.

Joseph had a lot of money and the opportunity to enjoy

life in unhealthy ways, yet he stayed the course. Instead of becoming indulgent like King Solomon, he remained true to who he had always been.

In Genesis 50:15–16, following Jacob's death, the brothers sent a message to Joseph. They were worried that after all the years, Joe was just faking forgiveness! They assumed that with their father gone, Joseph would change the way he treated them. When their message came to Joseph asking him to have mercy on them, it broke his heart. Verse 17 says that Joseph wept. He continued his love and forgiveness of his brothers, and he blessed them.

Though Joseph was absorbed in the Egyptian culture, he never forgot where he came from and the promises God had made about the future. In Genesis 50:24–25, Joseph made his family promise to take his remains back to Canaan. He knew Egypt wasn't his home, so he wanted his final act to be returning to his birthplace, forever sealing his message of forgiveness and reconciliation. He made a statement, and it was this: "I may be rich and famous, but I'm an Israelite, and I know that God has promised a land for us."

Joseph's faith is mentioned in the New Testament, in Hebrews 11:22. "By faith Joseph, when his end was near, spoke about the exodus of the Israelites from Egypt and gave instructions about his bones."

The writer of Hebrews doesn't mention Joseph's faith throughout his trials, his positive attitude, his withstanding temptation in Potiphar's house, or his ability to interpret dreams. Think about this. The greatest expression of Joseph's faith—the one worth mentioning in the New Testament—came at the end of his life. Despite all that had happened and all he had been through, Joseph didn't forget that he belonged to God.

Continuing the Journey

In January of 1995, we moved to Downey, California. The church was great, the congregation was happy to have us there, and we found a home that would work well for our family of four. I imagined a nice, long partnership with the ministry there. That's what I had always wanted—to stay with a congregation for a long time and watch what Jesus would do in the lives of people throughout generations.

But shortly after we arrived, I got a call from a guy in Clovis, California. He was calling on behalf of a church that wanted me to be their preacher. I didn't even know where Clovis was!

I didn't want to go. We had barely unpacked from our move to Downey. There was no way I was moving again.

Somehow, they convinced us to come and visit. And boy, were they nice to us! Clovis was a growing city, right next to Fresno, and the church had just relocated and built a new worship center right in the middle of some new neighborhoods.

Suanne loved Clovis and tried to help me see that it would be a good place to raise our young family. I needed more convincing. Or a big shove from God. I called on some godly men to pray, and I began to pray. Though I wanted to hear from God, you know what I wanted Him to say? "Stay right where you are, David."

The Clovis church kept calling, each time sweetening

the deal. The godly men who prayed told me to stay. I wanted to stay. Suanne wanted to go.

The only thing I could think to do was to ask the Clovis church for something totally impossible and unreasonable, and then when *they* said no, that would be my answer from God!

The next call went something like this:

> Clovis church: David, we really want you to be our preacher. We're willing to do anything to make that happen.
>
> Me: Would you be willing to hire my dad, too?
>
> Clovis church: (Click.)

They hung up on me. No joke! I can imagine the discussion on the other end. "Can you believe the nerve of that guy, asking us to hire his dad, too? We can't afford that!"

I imagined me calling my dad and asking him to come to California. I figured he'd refuse, too, since the church he was pastoring at the time was getting ready to move to a more suitable location and building that would set it up for some serious growth.

But none of that happened. After the Clovis church got over their shock, they crunched some numbers, prayed, and called me back to offer me *and* my dad a job.

I called my dad, expecting *him* to hang up on me, but instead, he agreed to come and serve with me in Clovis.

Giving Him the Glory

G.I. Joe action figures were marketed as true American heroes. They were loyal from beginning to end, and were willing to take on any mission, no matter how difficult or confusing, if it glorified the boss (that was me). Joseph—the ultimate G.I. Joe—lived out this same system of loyalty and faith. He was up for any challenge God threw at him, trusting that in the end, God had a greater plan that would exceed Joseph's wildest dreams.

I, like Joseph, wanted to be faithful to God with my life. And now, after all the speedbumps and setbacks, He appeared to be throwing in a ricochet. *Bam!* You're in Downey. *Boom!* You're in Clovis. I felt a little like the ball in a pinball machine. And though it was difficult to say goodbye to my new congregation, I knew God was in it.

None of this was my idea! But through this little ricochet, God not only continued the fulfillment of my dream to be a preacher, He also remembered my desire to have my family all together. The Bible says, "Delight yourself in the LORD, and he will give you the desires of your heart" (Psalm 37:4).

Delighting in the Lord. That's what it's all about, isn't it? Honoring, loving, and serving the One who made you, knows you, and puts you in just the right places at just the right times to fulfill His purposes.

Toward the end of his life, the Apostle Paul wrote to his protégé Timothy:

I have fought the good fight, I have finished the race, and I have remained faithful. And now the prize awaits me—the crown of righteousness, which the Lord, the righteous judge, will give me on the day of his return.
—*2 Timothy 4:7–8 (NLT)*

God-Inspired Joseph started his life wearing a colorful, royal coat. He traded that for prison clothes. Then he ended up wearing an earthly crown—but all those adornments were temporary. It was his belief in a God-given dream, and his unwavering commitment to serve the Dream-giver that earned him his eternal crown of righteousness.

Half a Century of Blessings

I'm not sure where the last twenty-five years have gone. But I'm still in Clovis! My dad arrived a couple of weeks before I did, back in December of 1995, and since then we have partnered together to preach, teach, and outreach to the growing community of Clovis. Our family has enjoyed more blessings serving in this wonderful community and body of believers than I can count. When I try to count them, the tears come readily. Our boys grew up here and then left our nest to start families of their own.

My dad has suffered pretty much every health challenge you can imagine in the last decade, and even though his condition necessitates him living in a care facility, he insists on getting out every weekend to come and greet the family of God at CrossCity Christian Church.

My mom recently moved in with Suanne and me. It's like old times! What a blessing it is to see her every day and enjoy the family connection that God established when I was a kid in Kansas.

Drew and his wife live in town with my beautiful, feisty, two-year-old granddaughter. And guess what? Another one is on the way! Drew maintains to this day that my dad is his favorite person of all time. I try not to be offended by that.

And just when I think God is done pouring on the blessings, He kicks in another one! As I write this, my youngest, Zach, is coming to town next month. He'll be serving on staff as our high school pastor. His wife will also be on staff in our Next Gen department.

I'm an emotional mess these days. But I think it's a good mess—and necessary! Life is precious, and our loved ones won't always be here with us. Life is unpredictable; we never know what is waiting around the corner. Life is God-given, so it's important to savor every moment, seize every opportunity, and not waste a second in giving thanks to the One who knows why we are here.

My prayer for you, friend, is that you will grab onto these truths and let them sink deep into your core—resulting in a life well-lived for your Creator. He has made you for a purpose, and He will guide you just as He did Joseph, and me. Start strong, continue strong, and finish strong!

WORKBOOK

Chapter Ten Questions

Question: Do you like to start projects? Do you also finish them? If not, why do you think you don't finish? How about your spiritual life? Where would you say you are in your journey? At the beginning (just getting to know God), in the middle (learning, growing, and seeking to be obedient to God's ways), or toward the end (you've walked many years with Jesus, but are eager to gain more wisdom and mentor others along their way)? What can you do today to take the next step in your journey?

Question: We live in a culture that no longer considers itself Christian. How does this affect you and your family in your day-to-day lives? Are you able to keep your eyes focused on God, or are you tempted to take the easy route and go with the flow? How can you strengthen yourself spiritually so you can better lead and serve your family in a pagan culture? How can you finish strong for the ones you love?

Question: Joseph went out of his way to honor his father and brothers, even after all that had happened. Is there someone in your family whom God is asking you to honor and care for, even though that family member has not honored you? Begin to pray about this, and see what happens.

Action: Begin to count your blessings. If you are a person who likes to journal, write them all down. Every day, take time to thank God for one of those blessings. This one small action will change your outlook on life. Then, begin to share how good God is with others. It will change their outlook, too!

CONCLUSION

I Am Not Joseph

Five-year-old David, who was mesmerized by the colorfully clothed flannel-board character at Sunday school, was on to something when he desired to be just like God-Inspired Joseph. Sounds so noble, doesn't it?

I am Joseph, and he is me.

Do I want to live my life like Joe did? For sure. Have there been parallels in our stories? Yes—speedbumps, setbacks, blessings, and all. Do I hope to be a spiritual superhero? Of course. Bring on the cape of many colors!

But the truth is: I am not Joseph. In fact, if there's a character I resemble *most* in the Joseph story, it's the brothers. I'm the brothers. And so are you.

You are probably thinking right now, "How can you say that? Joseph's brothers were jealous, proud, selfish, and just plain messed-up."

Yes. I know—it's a twist ending to this book! I had you all convinced I'm a modern-day Joseph, right? (Okay, maybe not.) But I wouldn't be able to call myself a preacher if I didn't tell you that the parallels are between

Joseph and *Jesus*. Not Joseph and me.

I mentioned it briefly in an earlier chapter. Joseph is often referred to as the Jesus of the Old Testament. Joseph's life provides valuable examples we can emulate, but many aspects of his story foreshadow the coming of the Messiah. Isn't that fascinating? Some scholars count close to one-hundred parallels.

Now you want to go back and read the story again, right? Do it! It will take on a totally new meaning.

But first let's go back to the brothers. Their selfishness and pride caused them to reject Jacob's favored son. Likewise, our selfishness and pride can cause us to reject God's son, Jesus Christ. And if we don't reconcile with God through Jesus, we'll be separated from Him for eternity.

> *For everyone has sinned; we all fall short of God's glorious standard. Yet God, in his grace, freely makes us right in his sight. He did this through Christ Jesus when he freed us from the penalty for our sins.*
> **—Romans 3:23–24** *(NLT)*

Joseph had to go to Egypt so he could save many people, including his brothers.

> *You intended to harm me, but God intended it for good to accomplish what is now being done, the saving of many lives.*
> **—Genesis 50:20**

Jesus went to the cross to make a way for you and me to be reconciled to God. That's what we refer to as being saved.

I tell you the truth, unless a kernel of wheat falls to the ground and dies, it remains only a single seed. But if it dies, it produces many seeds.

—*John 12:24*

Have you received new life through Jesus? Have you been baptized into Christ? If not, the offer is on the table! Jesus paid for you with His blood. He offers forgiveness, abundant joy, and eternal blessings freely, just like Joseph brought out the feast and the provisions for his brothers. All they had to do was humble themselves and receive. And all you must do is humble yourself and receive God's forgiveness and everlasting life. In this case, I would urge you, do what Joseph's brothers did!

You can begin your new life in Christ by praying something like this:

Lord, I come to you and ask you to forgive me, a sinner. I have been prideful and selfish, and I've gone my own way for much too long. I want to receive the new life you promise in Christ. I accept Jesus's death in my place, and I believe He rose again. I want to finish strong with Him at the center of my life, as my Lord and Savior. Thank you for your precious gift of eternal life.

In Jesus' name, amen.

Whether you have known Christ for a long time or you

just prayed the prayer above, my hope is that you will be inspired all the days of your life by everything you read in God's Word. The Joseph story is one of my favorite stories, but there are so many more. I also encourage you to be a part of a church family, where other believers can encourage you to walk every day of your life in God's truth. We all need each other!

My Sunday school teacher was right. Joseph had quite a story. But we all have a story, too, and we know the ending is spectacular, because we're all part of His story. So, take the next step toward Him today—and watch the blessings unfold.

About the Author

Born the youngest son of a preacher in Wichita, Kansas, David N. Rutherford has spent his life ministering throughout Texas, Oklahoma, Missouri, and now California. For the past two decades, David has been the senior pastor at CrossCity Christian Church in Fresno, CA. David is married to Suanne and is father to Drew and Zach.

About Sermon To Book

SermonToBook.com began with a simple belief: that sermons should be touching lives, *not* collecting dust. That's why we turn sermons into high-quality books that are accessible to people all over the globe.

Turning your sermon series into a book exposes more people to God's Word, better equips you for counseling, accelerates future sermon prep, adds credibility to your ministry, and even helps make ends meet during tight times.

John 21:25 tells us that the world itself couldn't contain the books that would be written about the work of Jesus Christ. Our mission is to try anyway. Because in heaven, there will no longer be a need for sermons or books. Our time is now.

If God so leads you, we'd love to work with you on your sermon or sermon series.

Visit www.sermontobook.com to learn more.

REFERENCES

Notes

[1] Strong, James. "G1377: dioko." *A Dictionary of the Words in the Greek Testament and the Hebrew Bible.* Faithlife, 2009.

[2] Strong, James. "H1681: dibbah." *A Dictionary of the Words in the Greek Testament and the Hebrew Bible.* Faithlife, 2009.

[3] "Joseph's Birthright Coat: Rediscovering Genesis 37 Through the Lens of Context." Preserving Bible Times. https://preserving bibletimes.org/wp-content/uploads/2014/03/Reflection.Joseph.pdf.

[4] Hasbro Toys. "G.I. Joe with Kung Fu Grip Commercial-70's-Hasbro Toys." YouTube video. March 30, 2013. https://www.youtube.com/watch?v=CPyq_Y6mSWQ.

[5] Strong, James. "H6117: Ya'aqob." *A Dictionary of the Words in the Greek Testament and the Hebrew Bible.* Faithlife, 2009.

[6] "Kung Fu Grip." Joepedia. https://gijoe.fandom.com/wiki/Kung_Fu_Grip.

[7] Wood, Robert W. "10 Notorious Tax Cheats: Queen of Mean Leona Helmsley Proved Little People Can Put You in Jail." *Forbes.* April

17, 2015. https://www.forbes.com/sites/robertwood/2015/04/17/10-notorious-tax-cheats-queen-of-mean-leona-helmsley-proved-little-people-can-put-you-in-jail/#69c641142d08.

[8] Taylor, Cameron C. "Lessons on Humility from the Life of Sam Walton." *Clever Dude.* May 26, 2009. https://cleverdude.com/content/lessons-on-humility-from-the-life-of-sam-walton/.

[9] Fadiman, Clifton and André Bernard, eds. "Albert Schweitzer." In *Bartlett's Book of Anecdotes.* Little, Brown and Company, 2000, p. 483.

[10] Sanders, J. Oswald. Quoted in Bob Russell, *Acts of God: Why Does God Allow So Much Pain?* Moody Publishers, 2014.

[11] Sophocles. "Oedipus Rex," scene 11. *The Oedipus Cycle: An English Version.* Houghton Mifflin Harcourt, 2002, p. 43.

[12] O'Reilly, Jane. "Isn't It Funny What Money Can Do?" March 30, 1986. *New York Times.* https://www.nytimes.com/1986/03/30/books/isn-t-it-funny-what-money-can-do.html.

[13] ten Boom, Corrie. "Guidepost Classics: Corrie ten Boom on Forgiveness." November 1972. In Guideposts. July 24, 2014. https://www.guideposts.org/better-living/positive-living/guideposts-classics-corrie-ten-boom-on-forgiveness.

[14] "Cheetah." National Geographic Kids. https://kids.nationalgeographic.com/animals/mammals/cheetah/.

Made in the USA
Middletown, DE
06 March 2021

34457394R00080